Contract Law in Finland

Contract Law in Finland

Second Edition

Petra Sund-Norrgård

This book was originally published as a monograph in the International
Encyclopaedia of Laws/Contracts.

Founding Editor: Roger Blanpain
General Editor: Frank Hendrickx
Volume Editor: Jacques Herbots

Published by:
Kluwer Law International B.V.
PO Box 316
2400 AH Alphen aan den Rijn
The Netherlands
E-mail: lrs-sales@wolterskluwer.com
Website: www.wolterskluwer.com/en/solutions/kluwerlawinternational

Sold and distributed by:
Wolters Kluwer Legal & Regulatory U.S.
7201 McKinney Circle
Frederick, MD 21704
United States of America
E-mail: customer.service@wolterskluwer.com

DISCLAIMER: The material in this volume is in the nature of general comment only. It is not offered as advice on any particular matter and should not be taken as such. The editor and the contributing authors expressly disclaim all liability to any person with regard to anything done or omitted to be done, and with respect to the consequences of anything done or omitted to be done wholly or partly in reliance upon the whole or any part of the contents of this volume. No reader should act or refrain from acting on the basis of any matter contained in this volume without first obtaining professional advice regarding the particular facts and circumstances at issue. Any and all opinions expressed herein are those of the particular author and are not necessarily those of the editor or publisher of this volume.

ISBN 978-94-035-4691-9

e-Book: ISBN 978-94-035-4452-6
web-PDF: ISBN 978-94-035-4882-1

The Author

 Petra Sund-Norrgård (born 1972) graduated from the University of Helsinki, Finland, as a lawyer (LLM) in 1996. She worked as an associate lawyer for what is now known as Roschier, Attorneys Ltd., for approximately five years (member of the Bar Association 2000–2001), and trained at bench for one year at District Court of Korsholm (1997–1998). In 2001 Sund-Norrgård switched to academia, first working as Assistant Professor of commercial law at Hanken School of Economics (2001–2009), and thereafter as a university lecturer at the University of Helsinki (2009–2017). During the period from September 2014– to August 2017, her position at the University of Helsinki was that of an Academy of Finland Postdoctoral researcher. In January 2018, Sund-Norrgård became professor in Commercial Law at Hanken School of Economics, and in March 2021, she became Professor of Law at the University of Helsinki. Sund-Norrgård became a licentiate of law in 2003, and in 2011 she obtained her doctorate in law (LLD), both at the University of Helsinki. In 2015 she became an adjunct professor (docent) of civil law, also at the University of Helsinki. Sund-Norrgård's fields of interest are contract law, intellectual property law and labour law.

The Author

Table of Contents

Table of Contents

Table of Contents

Table of Contents

List of Abbreviations

B2B Contract	Business-to-Business Contract
B2C Contract	Business-to-Consumer Contract
CISG	United Nations Convention on Contracts for the International Sale of Goods
CJEU	Court of Justice of the European Union
DCFR	Draft Common Frame of Reference
ECHR	European Court of Human Rights
FAI	The Finland Arbitration Institute
KKO	Korkein oikeus
MAO	Markkinaoikeus
NATO	North Atlantic Treaty Organization
PECL	Principles of European Contract Law
SOU	Statens Offentliga Utredningar
Unidroit Principles	Unidroit Principles on International Commercial Contracts
YSE 1998	Rakennusalan yleiset sopimusehdot, YSE 1998

List of Abbreviations

Preface

This monograph aims at giving the reader information on the main features of the Finnish contract law of today. Even though the discussion largely focuses on Finnish provisions, national case law and the legal writing of Finnish scholars, it is influenced by the fact that Finland has been a member of the European Union since 1995; the supremacy of EU law is thus recognized in Finland. Certainly, the ongoing harmonization of European contract law/civil law – for instance, in the form of the Principles of European Contract Law (PECL) and Draft Common Frame of Reference (DCFR) – is interesting also for Finland. An important international source of law is the United Nations Convention on Contracts for the International Sale of Goods (CISG), which entered into effect in Finland on 1 January 1989.

It is also of relevance to note the similarities that still exist between Finnish and Swedish law, which originate from the time Finland was an integral part of Sweden (from the late twelfth to the early nineteenth centuries). For Finland, as a Nordic country, the ongoing discussion on how to 'categorize' Nordic law is naturally an interesting one: Is Nordic law a separate legal family that can be placed somewhere between common law and civil law, albeit clearly leaning towards civil law? Despite the existence of numerous acts (statutes) in Finland, many questions are left to the courts. In addition, there is a strong focus on the balancing of interests, and general principles of contract law – developed in case law and legal writing – are recognized as sources of law. These aspects naturally impact the discussion.

Preface

General Introduction

§1. The General Background of the Country

1. Finland, officially the Republic of Finland, is situated in Northern Europe. It is a peninsula surrounded by the Baltic Sea with land borders with Sweden, Norway and Russia. In the south, there is a maritime border with Estonia.

2. Due to the fact that inland lakes and rivers make up 10% of the country, Finland is sometimes referred to as 'the land of the thousand lakes'. In addition, around 65% of the land area is covered in forest. The concept of 'Everyman's Right' ensures that you can walk freely in the forest enjoying mushrooms, berries and fresh air.

3. Finland, with its population of 5.5 million, is the most sparsely populated country in the European Union (EU); there are only sixteen inhabitants per square kilometre. The majority of the population is concentrated in the southern region, where also the capital and the largest city, Helsinki, is situated. Helsinki had a population of 656,920 at the turn of the year 2020, and over 1.5 million people live in the Greater Helsinki metropolitan area.

4. Of the world's capitals, only Iceland's Reykjavík lies more to the north than Helsinki, and Finland has a rather harsh climate with long winters. However, it is also affected by the Atlantic ocean current Gulf Stream. Consequently, due to the moderating effects of the Gulf Stream, the Baltic Sea and the inland lakes, the climate is relatively warm given the fact that Finland has the same latitude as the cold regions like Alaska, Siberia and southern Greenland. Due to the fact that a quarter of Finland's territory lies within the Arctic Circle, it is possible to experience the midnight sun during midsummer. At Finland's most northern point, the sun does not set for seventy-three consecutive days during summer and does not rise for fifty-one days during winter.

5. Culturally, Finland is an overall homogenous country with no sizeable immigrant population. Finland is, however, a bilingual country with two national languages, Finnish and Swedish. Finnish (in Finnish: *suomi*), along with, for example, Estonian and Hungary, belongs to the Finno-Ugrian or Uralic language family. As of 2020, the Finnish speaking population was 86.9% of all Finns. About 5.2% of Finns speak Swedish, which is a North Germanic language, as their first language. The general term Finland Swedish or Fenno-Swedish (in Swedish: *finlandssvenska,* in Finnish: *suomenruotsi*) may be used for the Standard Swedish and the dialects of Swedish that are spoken in Finland. It is a constitutional right of everyone to use his or her own language, either Finnish or Swedish, before courts of law and other authorities and to receive official documents in that language.[1] The third largest language in Finland is Russian, which is spoken by 1.5% of the population.

6. From the late twelfth to the early nineteenth centuries, Finland was an integral part of Sweden, which explains the official status of the Swedish language in Finland. In 1809, following the Swedish defeat in the so-called Finnish war between Sweden and Russia, Finland was incorporated into the Russian Empire as the autonomous Grand Duchy of Finland; the laws and constitution of Finland remained unchanged, but Finland still felt the autocracy of the tsar. Finally, following the 1917 Russian Revolution, Finland won its independence.

7. Already in 1918, Finland was divided by civil war. The opposing sides in this war consisted of the 'Reds', who were supported by the Soviet Union, and the 'Whites', who were supported by the German Empire. The conflict lasted from late January until mid-May 1918 and resulted in a victory for the 'Whites'. After a brief attempt to establish a kingdom, Finland became an independent democratic republic.

8. During World War II, Finland fought the Soviet Union twice: first in the Winter War of 1939–1940, and later in the Continuation War in 1941–1944. Finland lost land to the Soviets during that period of time, but it retained its independence.

9. As early as 1906, as the first nation in Europe, Finland gave the right to vote to all adult citizens, including women. In 1955, Finland joined the United Nations and established an official policy of neutrality. Finland is not a member of the military alliance, North Atlantic Treaty Organization (NATO), albeit today there is an open political debate on the topic of membership. Finland has freedom of religion, but 67.8% are members of the Lutheran National Church. Finland has been a member of the EU since 1995, and euro (EUR) has been the currency since 1999.

10. Finland was a relative latecomer to industrialization, remaining a largely agrarian country until the 1950s. Nowadays, Finland is a highly industrialized country whose economy relies heavily on exports. Finland's main trading partners are Germany, Sweden, Russia, China and the United States. Its most important branches of industry are forestry, technology, metals and metal products.

11. Finland is a sovereign republic. The Parliament, who represents the people, enacts legislation, approves the state budget, ratifies international treaties and oversees the Government, the members of which shall have the confidence of the Parliament.[2] Moreover, the Parliament elects the Prime Minister who directs the Government. The Parliament has two hundred members, who are elected for a term

---

1. Section 17 of the Constitution of Finland (731/1999).
2. Sections 1 and 2 of the Constitution of Finland.

of four years. Finland is a democracy with a strong multi-party system, and it is normal for multiple political parties to form coalition governments.

12. In Finland, the President of the Republic of Finland and the Government are the instances that exercise governmental powers.[3] The President is the nation's head of state, who leads the foreign policy, and is the commander-in-chief of the Defence Forces, which is responsible for the defence of Finland. Presidential elections are held in Finland every six years as direct, popular elections.

§2. LEGAL FAMILY

13. Finland can, perhaps with some hesitation, be defined as a continental civil law country, and historically the German influences have been noteworthy. For Finland, as a Nordic country, it is nonetheless important to note that it is possible to consider Nordic law to be a separate legal family that can be placed somewhere between common law and civil law. Although positioned between common law and civil law, at least Munukka finds Nordic law to be 'clearly leaning towards civil law'.[4]

14. There are no large, systematic private law codifications in Nordic law, and even though acts (statutes) certainly exist, many questions are left to the courts. Moreover, there is a strong focus on the balancing of interests, and general principles of contract law – developed in case law and legal writing – are recognized as sources of law. Despite this, the legal concepts are often clearly drawn from civil law traditions, many times with roots in the German Civil Code, BGB.[5] Before the 1980s, written law/legislation was of a limited significance in Finnish contract law, which is not really true anymore today: since the late 1980s, there has been a rather significant growth of legislation in Finnish contract law.[6]

§3. PRIMACY OF LEGISLATION

15. In Finland, legislation is the highest source of law. According to section 2 of the Constitution of Finland (731/1999), the exercise of public powers shall be based on an act, and in all public activity, the law shall be strictly observed.

16. According to a traditional Finnish doctrine of sources of law, these can be sorted into three groups in accordance with their binding effect: The strongly binding sources of law, the weakly binding sources of law and the permitted sources of law.

---

3. Section 3 of the Constitution of Finland.
4. Munukka 2015, 203.
5. Wilhelmsson et al. 2006, 28, Bernitz 1957–2010, 19–23 with reference to some European authors (Zweigert & Kötz; Arminjon & Nolde & Wolff; Tamm), Andersen & Runesson 2015, 15–16.
6. Hemmo 2008, 48.

17. The strongly binding sources contain statutory law and custom where there is no written law. Within the category of 'statutory law', the constitution is placed above 'normal' acts, and nowadays, the supremacy of EU law is recognized. In principle, this means that EU law even trumps the constitution, as does those general norms that are based upon case law from the Court of Justice of the European Union (CJEU). This is true also for the European Convention on Human Rights and those general norms that are based upon decisions of the European Court of Human Rights (ECHR).[7]

18. The category weakly binding sources are formed of court decisions – especially precedents by the Supreme Court – and legislative preparatory works. Lastly, the permitted sources contain, for example, legal writing (jurisprudence), general principles of law and 'real arguments' (in Finnish: *reaaliset argumentit*).[8]

§4. THE POSITION OF THE JUDICIARY

19. The judicial powers are exercised by – politically as well as otherwise – independent courts of law. The independence of the courts is guaranteed by the Constitution of Finland; the courts are only bound by the law in force.[9]

20. The general courts of law are the district courts, the courts of appeal and the Supreme Court.[10] They are organized in a three-level system, where the courts of first instance are the district courts. The district courts deal with criminal cases, civil cases and petitionary matters, such as divorce and custody of children. The courts of appeal function as appellate courts; a decision of a district court can be appealed in a Court of Appeal, albeit a leave for continued consideration is, with some exceptions, needed.[11]

21. The Supreme Court is the highest appellate court. In order to appeal a decision of a Court of Appeal in the Supreme Court, the Supreme Court must grant a leave to appeal. The purpose of the requirement of leave to appeal is to enable the Supreme Court to concentrate on guiding judicial practice through precedent.[12] For this reason, the courts of appeal are in practice the highest instances available for most court proceedings.

22. The task of the regional administrative courts and the Supreme Administrative Court is the judicial oversight of administrative acts. In cases that come before the administrative courts, one of the parties is a public authority who has made a decision with an impact on a citizen or a legal person, who then appeals the decision. In case the appellant is discontent with the decision of the administrative court,

---

7. Hirvonen 2011, 43.
8. Aarnio 2014, 230–232.
9. Section 3 of the Constitution of Finland.
10. Chapter 1, s. 2 of the Code of Judicial Procedure (4/1734, as amended 683/2016).
11. Chapter 25 a, s. 5 of the Code of Judicial Procedure (4/1734, as amended 386/2015).
12. Chapter 30 of the Code of Judicial Procedure (4/1734, as amended 104/1979).

it is possible to appeal further to the Supreme Administrative Court, or at least to apply to the Supreme Administrative Court for leave to appeal.[13]

23. There are also specialized courts, such as the Market Court and the Labour Court, with jurisdiction in certain areas. Leave of appeal – from the Supreme Court or the Supreme Administrative Court – is also required for appeal against decisions of the Market Court.[14] Based on section 36 of the Act on the Labour Court (646/ 1974), '[t]he judgment of the Labour Court is final and immediately enforceable in the same order as a final judgment of a general court of law'.[15]

24. The decisions of the Supreme Court and the Supreme Administrative Court, as well as the decisions of the European Court of Justice and the ECHR are considered to be precedents. Despite this, precedents are not as such legally binding but belong to the 'weakly binding' sources of law discussed above. In practice, the precedents are nonetheless of great importance. This is due to the fact that lower courts normally follow them in their work.

§5. Distinction Between Public Law and Private Law ('Administrative Contracts')

25. It is probably correct to say that Finland, as well as the other Nordic countries, belong to the 'civil law' culture.[16] In civil law, the distinction between public law and private law – as a starting point – is important. However, no comprehensive civil code exists in Finland; private law is instead codified in the form of statutes (acts). In addition, there are uncodified parts of private law in the form of general principles of law and the like.

26. Whereas private law deals with 'private matters', such as marriages or contracts, the role of public law has traditionally been to act as the guarantor of private rights against public power. It should nonetheless be stressed that the distinction between public law and private law is not as fundamental in Finland as in, for example, France or Germany. Moreover, due to the fact that some public duties are nowadays privatized, the distinction has perhaps lost even more of its original importance.[17]

---

13. Regional administrative courts, https://oikeus.fi/tuomioistuimet/en/index/tuomioistuinlaitos/ tuomioistuimet/hallintotuomioistuimet/hallinto-oikeudet.html and Supreme Administrative Court, https://www.kho.fi/en/index/organization.html. *See also*, for instance, the Act on Administrative Courts (430/1999), and the Administrative Judicial Procedure Act (808/2019).
14. Chapter 7 of the Market Court Proceedings Act (100/2013).
15. *See also* Labour Court of Finland, https://www.tyotuomioistuin.fi/en/index.html.
16. The slight hesitation here stems from the fact that Nordic law also can be defined as a separate legal family somewhere between common law and civil law.
17. Husa 2010, 4–5. For more detailed information on the division between, and content of, private and public law in Finland, *see* Toiviainen 2008, 57–60.

27. The term 'administrative contract' is used in the Administrative Procedure Act (434/2003). It is defined as 'a contract, within the competence of an authority, on the performance of a public administrative task, or a contract relating to the exercise of public authority'. The act in question requires that when such a contract is formed, 'the fundamental principles of good administration shall be adhered to' and, moreover, 'the rights of the persons concerned shall be adequately protected', as shall 'their chances to affect the contents of the contract' in the drafting phase.[18] In other words, the traditional idea of a need to protect private rights against the intrusion of public power is visible also here. It should be noted that in case of a dispute concerning an administrative contract, it shall, in accordance with section 66 of the Administrative Procedure Act (as amended 854/2020), be considered as a matter of administrative litigation in an administrative court.

28. In a discussion on the distinction between public law and private law, it could also be mentioned that Finland has undergone an extensive public procurement reform, which is based on the EU Directives on public procurement adopted in April 2014. An aim of the reform is, for instance, to simplify procurement procedures. As of 1 January 2017, the Act on Public Procurement and Concession Contracts (1397/2016) is in force.[19]

§6. DISTINCTION BETWEEN CIVIL LAW AND COMMERCIAL LAW ('COMMERCIAL CONTRACTS')

29. There is no sharp distinction in Finland between civil law and commercial law, and for example, the provisions of the Contracts Act (228/1929) apply to transactions between businesses as well as to transactions between natural persons. The same goes for the provisions of the Sale of Goods Act (355/1987). However, the provisions of the Sale of Goods Act are subject to the provisions of the Consumer Protection Act (38/1978). In other words, in those cases where businesses, for example, sell goods to consumers, the provisions of the Consumer Protection Act take precedence.

---

18. Section 3 of the Administrative Procedure Act (434/2003).
19. *See also* the information found at Ministry of Economic Affairs and Employment, Reform of Public Procurement Legislation, http://tem.fi/en/reform-of-public-procurement-legislation.

Introduction to the Law of Contracts

§1. Definition of Contract

30. In the Contracts Act (228/1929), one can find basic provisions on how to, for example, conclude a binding contract, but the said act does not present a definition of contract. It is also rather difficult to give a general definition of the concept.

31. As a starting point, there must be at least two parties to a contract, and in legal writing a contract has, for instance, been described as a combination of two or more legal/juridical acts, which presume each other.[20] In a more comprehensive manner, contract has been defined as 'a combination of two or several promises (transactions), through which the parties intentionally seek to a joint goal, with binding effect of the (rights and) obligations thus created, which are also enforceable and recognized by the law'.[21]

32. The word 'contract' can be used in at least three different ways. First, it may refer to the conclusion of a legally binding contract. Second, it may refer to the content of the relationship between the parties to the contract. In such a case, 'contract' refers to a number of rights and obligations between the parties. Third, the concept may be used as an equivalent to a certain contract document, which includes the contract clauses.[22] Hemmo, for example, underlines that it is a mistake to define a contract as nothing more than a certain contract document.[23]

33. The principle of freedom of contract is still the foundation of Finnish contract law. This is especially so for business-to-business contracts (hereinafter 'B2B contracts'). However, at times other concerns – such as competition law or the principle of loyalty (which has been viewed as a 'counter-principle' to freedom of contract)[24] – prevail.

34. In the case of business-to-consumer contracts (hereinafter 'B2C contracts'), mandatory provisions in the legislation often hinder the formation of contracts that deviate from the legislation to the detriment of the weaker party.

---

20. Saarnilehto et al. 2012, 309.
21. Toiviainen 2008, 73.
22. Saarnilehto et al. 2012, 310.
23. Hemmo 2008, 26.
24. Mäenpää 2010, 327 and references.

35. The principle of freedom of contract entails that individuals can choose whether or not to conclude a contract, with whom to conclude the contract and how to conclude the contract – for example, in writing or orally. The principle of freedom of contract also entails the essential right to decide the content of the contract in question. Especially for B2B contracts, the assumption is that the parties have had, and have used, their freedom of contract in the drafting process. Consequently, once a contract has been concluded, it is considered binding upon the parties (*pacta sunt servanda*). In Saarnilehto's words, the price of freedom of contract is the binding effect of contract.[25]

36. The binding effect is, for instance, limited by the general principle/ requirement of reasonableness found in section 36 of the Contracts Act (228/1929 as amended 956/1982), which makes it possible for a court or a court of arbitration to adjust unfair contract terms. It states: 'If a contract term is unfair or its application would lead to an unfair result, the term may be adjusted or set aside.' Section 36 can, however, only be applied by a court at the request of a party.[26]

37. The binding effect of contract has traditionally been explained through different theories. The basic idea of the so-called will theory is that a contractual obligation is based on a will to commit and an expression of this intent to the other contracting party. If the expression of intent for some reason differs from the actual will of its giver, the expression shall, however, not be binding. For this reason, the will theory is naturally problematic from the point of view of the other contracting party/the recipient and can rightfully be criticized for creating uncertainty. Consequently, the will theory has been followed by the so-called trust theory, which instead emphasizes the significance of the expression of intent as it may reasonably and objectively be understood. According to this theory, a bona fide recipient may trust the binding effect of an expression of intent. The provisions of the Contracts Act are mainly in line with the trust theory.[27]

38. In legal writing, for example, Hemmo has stressed the incorrectness of assuming that the binding effect of contract requires a clear intention to commit, as well as an explicit expression of such an intent.[28] The Supreme Court nonetheless stated in decision KKO 2011:6 – with reference to its earlier decision KKO 2006:71 – that a contract presupposes that a common intention among the parties concerning the will to form a contract, as well as concerning the content of the said contract, can be demonstrated. The Supreme Court moreover articulated that court practice, as well as legal writing, has adopted an attitude of reserve towards contracts not formed as a result of an express intent to commit. According to the Supreme Court, such an attitude is justified since it prevents that somebody is bound by a contract that he has neither accepted nor in some other way has expressed a desire to commit to. Despite this, it is rather clear that it may also in other situations be possible

---

25. Saarnilehto 2009, 38.
26. Government bill 247/1981, 16, Wilhelmsson 2008, 140.
27. Saarnilehto et al. 2012.
28. Hemmo 2008, 28.

to draw the conclusion that a contract has in fact been formed. Sometimes this can be done on the basis of the actions of the parties,[29] and sometimes due to passivity, perhaps in accordance with section 6(2) of the Contracts Act.

39. Section 6 of the Contracts Act, in its entirety, states: '(1) A reply that purports to be an acceptance but which, due to an addition, restriction or condition, does not correspond to the offer, shall be deemed a rejection constituting a new offer. (2) However, the provision in paragraph (1) shall not apply if the offeree has considered the reply to correspond to the offer and the offeror must have understood the same. If the offeror in that case does not wish to accept the reply, he/she shall, without undue delay, notify the offeree thereof; otherwise a contract shall be deemed concluded on the terms contained in the reply.' It can be noted in connection herewith that Finnish contract law differs from common law as no consideration (or similar) is required in order for a contract to become legally binding.

§2. HISTORICAL BACKGROUND OF THE LAW OF CONTRACTS

40. Sweden and Finland were one country until 1809. Although Finland was then separated from Sweden and made a Grand Duchy of Russia, Finland was permitted to keep its legal system, which self-evidently was fully identical with the Swedish one.[30] Thus, the current Finnish legal system originates from the Swedish General Code of 1734. This is a code formally still in force, although most of the material content of the same has gone through renewals and has been replaced with newer legislation.

41. Despite the fact that Finland and Iceland are republics, while Sweden, Norway and Denmark are monarchies, there are many cultural, as well as other, similarities among all the Nordic countries. This is true also for the law: Although it is probably correct to categorize Finland as a continental civil law country, it is possible to view Nordic law as a separate legal family. This question was already briefly illuminated above (*see* General Introduction, §2).

42. One of the special features of Nordic law, namely the lack of a systematic, comprehensive codification of private law, can be noted here again: The Nordic attitude towards codification has traditionally been – and is still – quite different compared to continental systems. Although the existing acts (statutes) certainly cover basic, important aspects of private law, they are not intended to be complete. Despite the fact that there, for example, is a special Contracts Act in force in all the Nordic countries, it does not nearly cover all aspects of contract law. In addition, the Contracts Act is old: it entered into force in Sweden, Denmark and Norway

---

29. Hemmo I 2003, 171–172, 606.
30. Bernitz 1957–2010, 16.

between 1915 and 1918, and in Finland in 1929. Due to the fact that there have been only a few amendments to the original text, some scholars find the Contracts Act to be outdated and partly obsolete.[31]

43. The Sale of Goods Act (355/1987) is also the result of Nordic cooperation. The 'old' Nordic Sale of Goods Acts, enacted between 1905 and 1922 were reformed through a rather lengthy process initiated by Finland in 1961 and leading up to the enactment of the new Sale of Goods Acts in Finland, Sweden and Norway between 1987 and 1990. (Denmark chose not to enact a new Sale of Goods Act.) The old Sale of Goods Act has traditionally – through analogies – largely functioned as a model in the development of Nordic contract law. To some degree, the Sale of Goods Act of today still has this function in Finnish contract law.[32]

44. It is worth mentioning that to this day there is legislative cooperation among the Nordic countries, although the inter-Nordic legal coordination has been in decline since the 1970s.

§3. CLASSIFICATION OF CONTRACTS

45. Contracts can be classified in many ways, for instance, according to types, such as contracts of sale, lease or agency. Many such specific contracts are discussed below in Part II of this monograph.

46. Another possibility is to classify contracts according to their general properties. Thus, contracts can, for example, be classified according to their duration (short-term or long-term contracts), the way in which the contract terms were formulated (standard terms or individually negotiated terms), or the nature of the parties to the contract (equal or not). One may also distinguish between unilateral and bilateral contracts.[33] These selected classifications – one can certainly also find others – are briefly discussed next.

47. The classification of contracts *according to their duration* does not produce a clear-cut dichotomy; many contracts can be placed somewhere between the following two extremes: One can be described as a short-term contract in the form of a discrete transaction comprising a single exchange after which no continuous legal relationship remains between the contracting parties. Liability for defects may however arise at a later stage if a performance is not in accordance with the agreed. A typical discrete transaction is a sale in a store, where one party is handed goods in exchange for money.

---

31. For some information, *see* for example Andersen & Runesson 2015, 18. A Swedish initiative to replace the old Nordic Contracts Act can be found at https://www.avtalslagen2020.se/.
32. Wilhelmsson et al. 2006, 28.
33. Saarnilehto et al. 2012, 316.

48. The other extreme in such a classification consists of a long-term, continuous cooperative arrangement based on trust where the input of both parties is needed in order to reach a common goal. In order to work well for the parties, such a contract should include enough flexibility, for instance, in the form of clauses on renegotiation and hardship. This makes it easier to prepare for the future and those changes in circumstances that inevitably will occur during the long contract term.[34]

49. Long-term contracts may be concluded for a fixed term or be open-ended/concluded until further notice. A contract with no fixed term is normally considered to be open-ended. In Finland, a party may, as the main rule, terminate such an open-ended, often long-term contract at any time by giving a reasonable period of notice, as long as this right is not limited in the law or in the agreement itself.[35]

50. Parties to long-term cooperation contracts are moreover generally expected – at least to some extent – to take also the other party's interests into consideration when fulfilling the contract. Consequently, for example, the principle of loyalty (good faith) has a greater impact on the interpretation of such contracts than on the interpretation of short-term discrete transactions.[36] Examples of long-term contracts are licensing, agency and franchise contracts.

51. Contracts may be classified *based on the way in which the contract terms are worked out/formulated*. In the case of an individually negotiated contract, the contracting parties have separately negotiated and agreed upon the terms for the contract in question. Another possibility is to conclude a contract on the basis of a set of pre-formulated standard terms. Due to the fact that standard terms make contract formation both faster and more affordable, they are widely used in business. The terms of economically very valuable contracts are nonetheless still usually negotiated individually by the parties.[37]

52. Standard terms may be problematic in situations where the contracting parties do not have equal bargaining power when the contract is to be concluded, that is, in situations where one party is significantly (for instance, economically) weaker than the other. A consumer or a small entrepreneur – such as a franchisee – concluding a contract with a large company can be mentioned as examples. Thus, in a situation where the standard terms are formulated by the strong party alone, he self-evidently has a significant advantage.

53. Standard terms can certainly also be formulated by both parties or by professional and industrial organizations representing the parties. In case of such agreed documents, the likelihood of balanced terms is naturally greater.

---

34. *See*, for example, Hemmo I 2003, 33–35, Hemmo II 2003, 375, Sund-Norrgård 2011, 283–284 Summary in English under the headline 'drafting and interpreting licensing agreements'.
35. Hemmo II 2003, 375–385, Sund-Norrgård 2012, 244.
36. Sund-Norrgård 2011, 56 and references to Finnish and Swedish legal writing.
37. Saarnilehto et al. 2012, 316–317.

54. Special principles – for instance, on how to conclude contracts that include standard terms – as well as for the interpretation of such contracts have been developed in legal writing and case law.[38] This issue is discussed further below (*see* Part I, Chapter 1, §1, I).

55. The nature of the contracting parties can be of great importance; a clear distinction is, for instance, made between B2C contracts and B2B contracts. A B2C contract is concluded between a business and a consumer, typically on the sale of goods or services, where the business is the seller and the consumer is the buyer. In the said contractual relationship, the consumer is considered to be the weaker party. The consumer's position is thus protected by mandatory provisions in the Consumer Protection Act (38/1978). This is an act that, according to Chapter 1, section 1(1), 'applies to the offering, selling and other marketing of consumer goods and services by businesses to consumers'. Contract terms that differ from such mandatory legislation to the detriment of the consumer shall be invalid (Chapter 5, section 2, as amended 16/1994).

56. The definition of a business in Chapter 1, section 5 of the Consumer Protection Act (as amended 16/1994) is 'a natural person or a private or public legal person who, in order to obtain income or other economic benefit, deals in, sells or otherwise offers consumer goods or services on a professional basis and for consideration', whereas a consumer, in Chapter 1, section 4 (as amended 16/1994) is defined as 'a natural person who acquires consumer goods and services primarily for a use other than business or trade'. Chapter 1, section 3 (as amended 16/1994) can be noted too. It defines consumer goods and services as 'goods, services and other merchandise and benefits that are offered to natural persons or which such persons acquire, to an essential extent, for their private households'.

57. The field of application of the Consumer Protection Act was discussed in Supreme Court decision KKO 2008:107. In this case, a management consulting company had sold a horse to a consumer. According to the trade register, the company's line of business included ownership of horses. The company had nevertheless not previously sold any horses or any other consumer goods either, and the activity in question was thus not found to be professional. Consequently, as regards the sale of the horse, the Supreme Court found that the company had not acted in the capacity of a business in the way that this concept is understood in the Consumer Protection Act.

58. It should be stressed that the Consumer Protection Act is not applicable where the contract is concluded between two natural persons or where a consumer is the seller and a business is the buyer of goods or services.

59. Since a B2B contract is concluded between two businesses who, as a starting point, are assumed to be equal, the parties may determine the contents of their contract rather freely. The contract may, for instance, include high-risk terms. The

---

38. For a comprehensive overview with examples from case law, *see* Wilhelmsson 2008, 65–98.

consequences of breaches of contract are more severe, and the threshold for contract adjustment is usually considerably higher in such contracts compared to B2C contracts.[39]

60. During the last decades, there has been an increased focus on the protection of the weaker party in Finnish contract law. Contract law has developed mostly in the area of consumer contracts and similar contract types, such as contracts on employment and residential leases. One may therefore conclude that 'the socialization of contract law' – at least to some extent – is a fact in Finland.[40]

61. Also, the so-called regulation of contract terms (in Finnish: *sopimusehtojen sääntely*) can be shortly addressed here. This is 'collective' interference by authorities in such contract terms – in practice standard terms – that are intended to be used in many contractual relationships. For B2C contracts Chapter 3 of the Consumer Protection Act is relevant. Chapter 3, section 1(1) states: 'A business offering consumer goods or services shall not make use of a contract term which, considering the price of the good or service and the other relevant circumstances, is to be deemed unfair from the point of view of consumers.' In cases like these, the question of possible unfairness of a contract term is not tried as a separate contractual dispute in the general court. Instead, it is the Market Court and the Consumer Ombudsman[41] that issue necessary injunctions.

62. According to Chapter 3, section 2(1) of the Consumer Protection Act, where it is necessary in respect of consumer protection, 'a business may be enjoined from continuing the use of a contract term contrary to section 1(1) or repeating the use of such a term or a comparable term'. Moreover, unless this is deemed unnecessary, the injunction shall be reinforced by the threat of a fine (as amended 1259/1994).

63. Based on Chapter 3, section 3 of the Consumer Protection Act (as amended 684/2012), an injunction of the kind referred to in section 2 shall be issued by the Market Court, which may also issue an interim injunction. However, in some cases also, the Consumer Ombudsman may issue an injunction or an interim injunction referred to in section 2.[42]

64. Even though contracts are usually *bilateral*, and thereby creating reciprocal obligations for both parties, a contract can also be *unilateral*, and thus creating obligations only for one of the parties. The guaranty can be mentioned as an example of the latter type of contract. Based on section 2(1) of the Act on Guaranties and

---

39. Hemmo I 2003, 31–32.
40. Saarnilehto et al. 2012, 317–318.
41. Information on the Consumer Ombudsman is found at the website of the Finnish Competition and Consumer Authority https://www.kkv.fi/en/about-us/the-consumer-ombudsman/.
42. The provisions of Ch. 3 of the Consumer Protection Act were applied in, for instance, Market Court decisions MAO 186/10, MAO 1995:017, MAO 1991:012, MAO 120/06, MAO 1985:13, MAO 10/21, and MAO 146/21. *See also* Supreme Court decision KKO 2016:49. In addition, *see* the discussion in Sund-Norrgård 2014, 42–51, where also the regulation of B2B contracts – in order to protect small businesses – is discussed.

Third-Party Pledges (361/1999), it is defined as 'an undertaking where the undertaking party (guarantor) promises to answer for the repayment of another person's
(debtor) obligation (principal debt) to a creditor'.[43]

§4. CONTRACT AND TORTS

65. Contractual liability for damages is to be separated from non-contractual/
delictual liability for damages. The Tort Liability Act (412/1974), providing general
provisions on liability for damages, is applicable only to the latter type: According
to Chapter 1, section 1 of the said act, it 'does not apply to liability for damages
under contract'. As a main rule, a person is liable in accordance with the Tort Liability Act if he or she 'deliberately or negligently causes injury or damage to another'
(Chapter 2, section 1).

66. As for non-contractual liability for damages, the distinction between compensation for personal injury, damage to property and compensation for economic
loss that is not connected to personal injury – that is pure economic loss – is a rather
important one. For instance, based on Chapter 5, section 1 of the Tort Liability Act
(as amended 509/2004), compensation for pure economic loss is possible only
'[w]here the injury or damage has been caused by an act punishable by law or in
the exercise of public authority, or in other cases, where there are especially weighty
reasons for the same'.

67. In case of contractual liability for damages, such a separation of different
types of injuries is not as important: It is possible to be awarded compensation for
any of the three types of losses without the need to establish the existence of special
conditions of the kind required in the Tort Liability Act. Contractual liability is actually, in reality, mostly focused on the protection of economic interests; personal
injury and damage to property are less typical.[44]

68. The Tort Liability Act will not be discussed further, as will not those special
acts that regulate specific types of delictual liability for damages.[45]

69. Liability for damages is an important remedy in case of delay, defective performance or other breaches of contract. There is no act in Finland that provides general provisions for contractual liability for damages. Such liability is instead
regulated in acts applicable to specific contracts,[46] and many issues in connection

---

43. *See also* Saarnilehto 2009, 8.
44. Hemmo II 2003, 251–251.
45. *See* Saarnilehto et al. 2012, 499 for a few examples.
46. Hemmo 1998, 28–29.

with contractual liability for damages are to be solved on the basis of general principles of contract law. This is due to the fact that not all specific contracts are regulated in special acts. Moreover, not all special acts include provisions for liability for damages.[47]

70. In case of breach of contract, the aggrieved party is usually to be compensated with a sum that will put him as nearly as possible into the hypothetical position he would have been in had the contract been duly performed, that is in accordance with the so-called positive interest (in Finnish: *positiivinen sopimusetu*). Another, more limited, possibility is to be compensated in accordance with a hypothetical situation in which no preparation for contract formation has taken place, that is in accordance with the so-called negative interest (in Finnish: *negatiivinen sopimusetu*). Although the Finnish system for compensation is of German origin, the first alternative can be said to correspond to the English so-called expectation interest, the second to the so-called reliance interest.[48]

71. Negligence (or *culpa*) is the main rule not only for delictual liability for damages but for contractual liability for damages as well. However, in case of contractual liability for damages, the reversed burden of proof is the norm. In other words, although negligence is the basis for liability, the existence of a breach of contract in itself indicates that the party in breach has acted negligently. Thus, he is free from liability only if he proves that he has acted diligently or that he is not responsible for the event causing the loss.[49]

72. There are also other possibilities. For example, the Sale of Goods Act (355/1987) distinguishes between liability for direct loss and liability for indirect loss due to breach of contract. The damages for direct loss are based on the so-called principle of control liability. The said principle entails that liability for loss arises unless it is shown that the event that caused the loss has not been within the party's sphere of control. This can be illustrated with section 27(1) of the Sale of Goods Act that deals with the seller's control liability in case of delay. It states: 'The buyer is entitled to damages for losses that he suffers because of the seller's delay in delivery, unless the seller proves that the delay was due to an impediment beyond his control which he could not reasonably be expected to have taken into account at the time of the conclusion of the contract and whose consequences he could not reasonably have avoided or overcome.'[50]

73. Liability for indirect loss is based on negligence. This is made clear in section 27(4) of the Sale of Goods Act, which states: 'The buyer is always entitled to damages, including indirect losses, if the delay or loss is due to negligence attributable to the seller.'

---

47. Saarnilehto et al. 2012, 499.
48. Hemmo 1998, 148–149, Hemmo II 2003, 260–261.
49. Mononen 2004, 1389.
50. *See also* s. 40(1) on the seller's control liability for losses that the buyer suffers because of a defect in the goods.

74. In some situations strict liability is applied. This means that a person is legally responsible for the damage and loss caused by his acts and omissions regardless of negligence.[51] In addition, liability without exception (in Finnish: *poikkeukseton vastuu*) is a possibility. This means that liability is not exempted even in case of force majeure and similar (as is the case where strict liability is applied).[52]

75. Chapter 5, section 20(1) of the Consumer Protection Act (38/1978, as amended 16/1994) on the seller's liability for the consumer's direct loss in case of a defect in the goods, can be mentioned as an example of liability without exception. It states: 'The buyer shall be entitled to compensation for loss that he/she suffers because of a defect in the goods.' Liability for the consumer's indirect loss in case of a defect in the goods, however, requires negligence.

76. The impact of a warranty given by the seller should be noted. For instance, section 40(3) of the Sale of Goods Act states: 'The buyer is always entitled to damages, including indirect losses, if the defect or loss is due to negligence attributable to the seller or if the goods did not, at the time of the conclusion of the contract, conform to an express warranty of the seller.' This means that liability for damages in case of a warranty does not presuppose argumentation based on seller's negligence; instead liability can, in these cases, be based directly on the fact that such a warranty has been given.[53]

77. Especially, in case of B2B contracts, the importance of the parties' freedom of contract should be stressed.[54] For instance, contracts often include different kinds of limitation of liability clauses. The purpose of such clauses may be to reduce the liability for damages in different ways. One can, for example, use maximum liability caps or exclude liability for certain types of damages, such as indirect loss. In most cases, limitation of liability clauses are legally binding. They may nonetheless lose their effect due to gross negligence or because the clause is deemed unfair based on section 36 of the Contracts Act (228/1929, as amended 956/1982).[55]

78. Naturally, a clause in a B2C contract that restricts the consumer's right to damages shall be invalid if it is contrary to mandatory provisions of the Consumer Protection Act.

§5. CONTRACT AND QUASI-CONTRACT

79. In common law, the term 'quasi-contract' was historically used for legal actions for the recovery of money, while a more modern approach uses the term for

---

51. Mononen 2004, 1380.
52. Hemmo 1998, 39–41.
53. Wilhelmsson et al. 2006, 140.
54. Mononen 2004, 1381, 1388–1389.
55. Liebkind 2009, 127, Sund-Norrgård II 2015, 124–127.

a wider range of restitutionary actions.[56] In Finnish law, where obligations are mainly based on contract law or tort law, quasi-contract is not a legally defined concept. It is nonetheless a concept that is occasionally found in legal writing. For example, according to Saxén, it is at times possible that silent undertakings or contractual aspects – for which he uses the term 'quasi-contract' – can justify liability for damages in situations other than those which clearly qualify as contractual.[57]

80. The doctrine of *culpa in contrahendo* has by some scholars been defined as 'quasi-contractual' due to the fact that it has made it possible to consider a party contractually liable for damages in situations where no contract is yet concluded.[58]

81. The so-called *negotiorum gestio*, where a person, without proper authorization, performs necessary legal acts on behalf of an absent person, is known in Finnish law. The same goes for the doctrine of restitution of unjust enrichment, which according to Roman law was included in the concept of quasi-contract.[59] Restitution of unjust enrichment is a legal remedy by which the effects of unjustified performances may be eliminated in situations where contract law or tort law cannot be applied. Culpa in contrahendo, *negotiorum gestio*, as well as restitution of unjust enrichment are discussed in more detail below (*see* Part I, Chapter 1, §3, II, and Part II, Chapter 13, §1 and §2).

§6. CONTRACT AND THE LAW OF PROPERTY

82. The Finnish concept *esineoikeus* can literally be translated into 'the law of things/objects'. In other words, *esineoikeus* does not as such exist in common law. This follows from the fact that common law does not – unlike Germany and other Continental European countries – clearly differentiate between 'the law of things' and 'the law of obligations'. *Esineoikeus* is nonetheless roughly equivalent to the branch of law called the 'law of property'.[60]

83. In Finland, the law of property can first be defined as the branch of law that concerns ownership, as well as more limited rights in a subjective meaning to objects (traditional approach). Second, the law of property can be defined as the branch of law that deals with problems in connection with the protection of a third party in the exchange (a more modern approach). Today, the branch of law called the law of property is perhaps most rightfully placed somewhere in between these two definitions: On the one hand, it is concerned with questions related to the authority over objects and their usage, and on the other, it is concerned with questions related to the protection of third parties in the exchange.[61]

---

56. Sullivan 1975, 2.
57. Saxén 1975, 75.
58. Vedenkannas 2009, 980–981.
59. Norros I 2012, 10 and references, Saarnilehto et al. 2012, 44.
60. Saarnilehto et al. 2012, 44.
61. Kartio 1998, 1057–1058, Saarnilehto et al. 2012, 719–722, Kaisto 2016, 8–9.

84. Within the law of property, a thing/object is normally understood as an individualized, tangible object that can be at a person's disposal. Conventional examples of such objects are a book and a car. A document, such as a contract of sale or a share are also objects despite the fact that their legal relevance has more to do with the written content of them than with their physical attributes. For example, an individualized batch of potatoes, or a certain barrel of oil, are considered objects as well. Another very important category is real property. In the prevailing system, the law of property is not applied to intangibles, such as debts/claims or intellectual property rights (IPRs) (patents, trademarks and the like).[62]

85. The law of property has several connections to contract law. Many rights – ownership as well as more limited rights – are often based on a contract. That contract thus has a decisive impact on the content of the said right. Contracts can moreover be decisive in the separation of different rights from each other. In other words, the different types of rights (ownership, right to usage, pledge, etc.) are often defined on the basis of contracts.

86. Kartio stresses that the law of property is not enough when one tries to solve problems of today; contract law is often needed as well. However, contract law and the law of property have their own roles in terms of resolving problems in relation to exchange: While contract law mainly aims to provide a solution to questions concerning the relationship between the contracting parties (*inter partes*), the law of property focuses on the protection of a third party and on the *ultra partes* effects of legal acts. One may not, for instance, through contract alone decide on the dynamic protection of the third party in case of a collision between several rights. Thus, it is often dependent on the point of view, whether one focuses on contract law aspects or law of property aspects of a certain right.[63]

87. It can be noted that Finnish contract law does not recognize the common law distinction between legal ownership and equitable ownership; In Finland you are either the owner or you are not (joint ownerships are nonetheless possible).

§7. CONTRACT AND TRUST

88. Trusts in the form known in common law – that is a fiduciary relationship that allows a third party, the trustee, to hold assets on behalf of another person, the beneficiary – do not as such exist in Finnish law. The foundation (in Finnish: *säätiö*), which in short will be discussed here, can nonetheless be said to be an equivalent of the British 'charitable trust' and the American 'non-profit foundation' and 'private foundation'.[64]

---

62. Tepora 2009, 46–47.
63. Kartio 1998, 1062–1063, Tepora 2009, 37–45. *See also* Tammi-Salminen 2010, who discusses 'contract and the third party' as a theme that connects contract law and the law of property.
64. Association of Finnish Foundations, About Finnish Foundations, https://saatiotrahastot.fi/en/tietoa-saatioista-eng/.

89. In Finland, a foundation can be established using a charter or with a testamentary disposition; in both procedures the foundation – that must have a basic capital of at least EUR 50,000 – is considered established when it is entered in the Register of Foundations. Registered foundations are legal persons set up to manage property donated for a particular purpose. The purpose in question, which is to be determined when setting up the foundation, must be beneficial for society: It can be to provide funding for art, culture or science or to produce wellbeing services. The task for the foundation's management is to carefully further the foundation's purpose and promote its interests.

90. The Foundations Act (487/2015) entered into force on 1 December 2015. It replaced the previous Act from the 1930s, and was enacted in order to strengthen the supervision of foundations and increase the transparency of their activities. The act includes a number of new details that have to be registered with the Finnish Patent and Registration Office.[65]

91. A foundation can conclude contracts. The right for a foundation – with its beneficial purpose – to engage in business activities is, however, regulated in Chapter 1, section 7 of the Foundations Act. In short, a foundation's business operations have to serve the main purpose of the foundation. In terms of liability to pay taxes, a foundation must, for instance, pay income tax for business income and real estate income if the real estate is not used for a common or charitable purpose.[66]

92. There are provisions in the Foundations Act on bias/conflict of interest in the conclusion of contracts: For example, according to Chapter 3, section 4, a board member of the foundation shall not participate in the preparation, processing or decision-making for a matter if it concerns a contract or legal issue between the foundation and the person in question, or if the said board member otherwise anticipates an essential benefit that may be in conflict with the foundation's benefit.

93. A foundation is expected to prepare guidelines on the extended list of so-called related parties[67] applicable to its operations. Such guidelines should, among other things, include the process regarding handling and decision-making concerning commercial and other contracts for related parties in order to avoid conflicts of interest. The starting point is that related parties to the foundation should avoid contractual commitments with the foundation altogether. Should the benefit of the foundation nonetheless require contracts of this kind, the board of directors is to demonstrate that they serve the foundation's benefit. Contracts and business transactions with related parties are moreover mainly made based on market prices. And although the foundation is allowed to outsource operations related to operative

---

65. For additional information, *see* for example Finnish Patent and Registration office, https://www.prh.fi/en/saatiorekisteri.html, and Investment and Pensions Europe, Finnish foundation law set to strengthen governance, https://www.ipe.com/countries/nordic-region/finnish-foundation-law-set-to-strengthen-governance/10011117.article.
66. *See* Association of Finnish Foundations, Good Governance of Foundations, https://saatiotrahastot.fi/wp-content/uploads/2021/05/SRNK_Good-Governance-of-Foundations.pdf, 36–37.
67. *See* Ch. 1, s. 8 for information on these related parties (in Finnish: *lähipiiri*).

activities and administration, responsibility for such operations cannot be transferred or externalized. Consequently, the separate contracts that are to be prepared for outsourcing will also be closely monitored.[68]

§8. GOOD FAITH AND FAIR DEALING

94. The lack of complete acts in Finnish contract law leaves room for other sources of law; for example, general principles of contract law are recognized as sources of law. According to the prevailing paradigm in Finnish law, norms can be divided into rules and principles. Rules are applicable in an all-or-nothing fashion. A conflict between two rules thus means that only one of the conflicting rules may be applied in a given situation. A principle is more abstract in comparison to the rule and it can be applied to a greater or to a lesser extent. In the case of conflicting principles, the sphere of applicability in the situation at hand is resolved through 'weighing and balancing'. A principle, which is acceptable according to the values of society, is considered to be a general principle of law.[69]

95. The so-called principle of loyalty is a general principle of contract law. It can be described as the Finnish/Nordic equivalent of the principle of good faith (or *Treu und Glauben* or *bonne fois*) in the civil law countries of Continental Europe. These are all based on the Roman law idea that parties to a contract to some extent must take the other party's interests into consideration.[70]

96. Taxell introduced the principle of loyalty in Finnish legal writing already in the 1970s.[71] The discussion on contract as cooperation, and the importance of the principle of loyalty in that context, took off in the 1990s. The principle of loyalty has since then been extensively discussed in Finnish legal writing.

97. The principle of loyalty cannot as such be found in any acts in Finland. Pros and cons of a codification have been discussed over the years. The principle of loyalty can, however, be found in 'the background' of many legal rules. As examples, one can mention two sections of the Contracts Act (228/1929). The first one is section 33, based on which 'honour and good faith' is a prerequisite for the conclusion of a binding contract. It states: 'A transaction that would otherwise be binding shall not be enforceable if it was entered into under circumstances that would make it incompatible with honour and good faith for anyone knowing of those circumstances to invoke the transaction and the person to whom the transaction was directed must be presumed to have known of the circumstances.' The second one is section 36 (as amended 956/1982), which expresses the principle of reasonableness

---

68. For this, as well as additional, information on the subject, *see* Association of Finnish Foundations, Good Governance of Foundations, https://saatiotrahastot.fi/wp-content/uploads/2021/05/SRNK_ Good-Governance-of-Foundations.pdf.
69. *See*, for example, the comprehensive discussion in Pöyhönen 1988, 13–79. *See also* Aarnio 1989, 78–82, Tuori 2008, 55.
70. Munukka 2015, 203.
71. Taxell 1972 and Taxell 1977 are important in this context.

that allows unfair contract terms to be adjusted or even set aside. It states: 'If a contract term is unfair or its application would lead to an unfair result, the term may be adjusted or set aside. In determining what is unfair, regard shall be had to the entire contents of the contract, the positions of the parties, the circumstances prevailing at and after the conclusion of the contract, and to other factors.' Both section 33 and section 36 of the Contracts Act can be described as codifications of a more common demand for fair, honest, moral and even ethical behaviour.

98. Today most scholars are of the opinion that the principle of loyalty exists in Finnish contract law, even though its content is somewhat vague, and its applicability is somewhat unclear. The situation is roughly the same also in the other Nordic countries.[72]

99. The principle of loyalty is mentioned in certain legislative preparatory works. For instance, Government bill 241/2006 describes section 33 of the Contracts Act as an expression of a general principle of loyalty, since it protects good faith and promotes openness: Even though each party to a contract, as a starting point, is to obtain the relevant information himself, a party is under the obligation to inform the other party of such essential, relevant issues that he (the other party) has no knowledge of. The parties to a contract are thus to make sure that there is no information asymmetry between them.

100. The principle of loyalty is also mentioned in court decisions; the Supreme Court occasionally makes a reference to the said principle in its work. The principle of loyalty nonetheless lacks the concretion of a rule, and its actual content, and its relevance is therefore dependent on the circumstances of the case at hand.

101. It is rather clear that the principle's main focus is 'procedural'. By this, I mean that it is not primarily focused on altering contract clauses (as section 36 of the Contracts Act). Instead, the principle of loyalty is more concerned with fostering the parties to a contract – especially parties to long-term cooperation contracts based on trust and interdependence – to behave towards each other in accordance with some sort of best practices.

102. It is to be stressed that the principle of loyalty not only exists in consumer contracts,[73] employment relations,[74] or fiduciary relations – such as agency contracts – but in licensing agreements, franchising agreements and other commercial cooperation contracts as well.[75] According to the rather recent Supreme Court decision KKO 2020:96, an agent had acted contrary to the principle of loyalty in the following situation. The agency contract had been terminated by the principal, and

---

72. *See* Munukka 2015, 215 who finds its position in Norwegian law to be more established and firm.
73. *See*, for example, Supreme Court decision KKO 2008:91.
74. *See*, for example, Supreme Court decisions KKO 2016:13, KKO 2016:15, and KKO 2020:74.
75. *See also* Munukka 2015, 209–213.

shortly thereafter, the agent had presented a machine that competed with the principal's machine. The agent had, in fact, developed and manufactured it during the term of the agency contract using technical solutions that were protected by the principal's utility model.

103. The principle of loyalty certainly also exists between the parties to the sale of goods contracts. In legal writing, several sections of the Sale of Goods Act (355/ 1987) have been connected with the principle of loyalty. Examples of such are sections that deal with honour and good faith, a duty to inform/notify the other party, mitigation of loss and preservation of the goods.[76] The short-term nature – in other words, the lack of a long-term relation between the parties – of these and similar transactions nonetheless makes it less important to focus on loyalty aspects.

104. The main function of the principle of loyalty is perhaps to act as support/a guiding principle in the interpretation of a contract. Its application may also result in the actual modification of explicit contract clauses. In addition, on the basis of the principle of loyalty, the parties to a contract can, for example, be expected to contact and inform each other, discuss problems, renegotiate the contract, keep secret information – and not compete with each other during the contract term. Such duties may or may not follow from express contract clauses. In other words, the principle of loyalty can be said to have a complementary function in case of gaps in the contract since it supplements the contract with obligations implied by law. This means that if the written contract lacks a clause as to renegotiation, duty to inform the other party, secrecy or non-competition, this does not, in itself, justify the conclusion that such obligations are not a part of the contract.[77] Since the principle of loyalty functions as a legal basis for the parties' legitimate expectations, the gaps of the contract can often be filled with what is perceived as 'normal' for the type of contract within the said trade. Because of this, the principle of loyalty may also support the parties' choice to conclude a flexible enough contract.[78] One may thus draw the conclusion that the principle of loyalty is essentially about cooperating fully with the other party and thereby contributing to the fulfilment of the common goal/ purpose of the contract.[79] Having said this, it is unclear to what extent implied obligations of this kind may be based on the principle of loyalty only in the Finnish contract law of today. It is moreover unclear whether it is to be considered a breach of contract – that, for instance, can give cause for payment of damages – if one acts contrary to the principle of loyalty.

105. The impact of the principle of loyalty is most prominent during the contractual phase. However, parties may to some degree be required to act in accordance with the principle of loyalty also during contract negotiations as well as in the termination phase of a contract. The Supreme Court stated in its decision KKO

---

76. Routamo 1988, 22–23.
77. Sund-Norrgård 2011, 78–79 and references.
78. Sund-Norrgård et al. 2015.
79. For different views in connection to this *see*, for example, Pöyhönen 1988, 19, Muukkonen 1993, Häyhä 1996, Sund-Norrgård 2011, 77.

2008:91 that parties who engage in contract negotiations are bound by a reciprocal duty to act loyally in such a way that the other party is not mistaken in terms of the contract's essential prerequisites or meaning.[80] Already in 1993, in decision KKO 1993:130, the Supreme Court referred to the principle of loyalty in terms of a duty to inform the other party of essential issues in the pre-contractual phase. This was the first time ever that the Supreme Court made a reference to the said principle in its work.

§9. STYLE OF DRAFTING

106. There is freedom of contract in Finland. This also includes freedom of form which, for instance, means that orally concluded agreements are usually just as valid as those concluded in writing.

107. It should be observed that freedom of contract also means that the contract parties are in fact free to decide upon requirements to form their particular contract. In practice, it is rather common that parties decide that their contract must be signed by both of them in order to be valid; in other words, the parties specifically agree that everything that happens before signing (in terms of discussions, e-mails, meetings, etc.) is part of the negotiation process only. It is also common to agree that inter-party notifications of delays and other difficulties and problems in the fulfilment of the contract are to be made in writing as well.[81]

108. Finnish contract law does not include a parol evidence rule or similar. Probably – at least in part – due to this, the style of drafting can generally be characterized as somewhat less 'wordy' in comparison to the Anglo-American style. Having said this, it should be observed that in some areas, such as contracts for mergers and acquisitions, the style of drafting is heavily influenced by the Anglo-American drafting style. Consequently, commercial contracts between two Finnish parties are sometimes not only drafted in English but may also be comprehensive and detailed, including whereas clauses, boiler plate-clauses and the like. Due to the influences of common law, one may also, for instance, find clauses on best efforts (best endeavours) in licensing agreements that fall under Finnish jurisdiction, despite the fact that this concept does not as such exist in Finnish contract law.[82]

109. Based on the so-called proactive contracting approach, which nowadays is visible also in Finnish legal writing, an '*ex ante*-take' on contracts/contracting is preferred. This is a view that stresses the importance of planning ahead, of discussions and cooperation *inter partes*, and the conclusion of contracts that actually work for the parties.[83] A long-term cooperation based on trust may thus benefit from

---

80. *See also* Supreme Court decision KKO 2007:72.
81. Norros 2008, 183.
82. *See,* for example, Sund-Norrgård 2011, 21, 161–167 and references.
83. *See,* for instance, the discussion in Sund-Norrgård 2011, 98–100, and Haapio 2013, 30–45.

a flexible, shorter contract due to the fact that the parties are more focused on reaching a common goal as smoothly as possible than on risk allocation.[84] Despite this, it nevertheless appears as if many long-term cooperation contracts in Finland are in practice still formed in a rather comprehensive and detailed style.[85]

110. Even though there is freedom of contract in Finland, form requirements have been imposed in the legislation for certain types of contracts. One such example is the marriage settlement which, based on Part II, Chapter 3, section 42 of The Marriage Act (234/1929, as amended 448/1999), is to be concluded in writing and registered by the District Court. It is made clear in section 44 of the said act (as amended 308/1986) that the marriage settlement does not take effect unless it is submitted to the court and properly registered.

111. A few of the provisions of the Code of Real Estate (540/1995) will be shortly discussed here too; the act in question is another example of such legislation that includes form requirements for contracts.

112. According to Chapter 1, section 1 of the Code of Real Estate, one may acquire title to real estate 'by sale, trade, gift or other conveyance, as provided in this Code'.[86] It is to be noted that the provisions of the code on the conveyance of real estate 'apply also to the conveyance of a share and a parcel of real estate, a common, a parcel and a share of a common' (Chapter 1, section 2).

113. Provisions on sales of real estate are found in Chapter 2. According to section 1, concerning the form of the deed of sale, '[a] sale of real estate shall be concluded in writing. The seller and the buyer or their attorneys shall sign the deed of sale. A notary shall attest the sale in the presence of all the signatories of the deed of sale'. Due to amendment 96/2011 to the Code of Real Estate, it is nowadays also possible to conclude sales of real estate electronically. In order to be valid, such a sale must nevertheless be handled through the nationwide electronic system regulated in Chapter 5 of the Code.

114. The Supreme Court decision KKO 2014:70 is an interesting one in connection with a discussion on sales of real estate. A couple had bought a real estate from another couple. Soon after the sale, defects were noticed in the object. Three months after the sale, the parties concluded a separate contract on the compensation (EUR 15,000 in all) to be paid by the sellers to the buyers. The contract also included a clause stipulating that the parties would not have any additional claims towards each other. About two years after the sale, the buyers demanded a price reduction in court. The sellers disputed the claim with reference to the above-mentioned contract. The Supreme Court found this contract to be such a, from the deed of sale, separate contract, the validity of which was *not* to be assessed based directly on the

---

84. Sund-Norrgård 2011, 100–103, Sund-Norrgård et al. 2015.
85. *See*, for instance, Sund-Norrgård 2011, 144 concerning licensing agreements.
86. This provision continues by stating: 'Separate provisions apply to the acquisition of real estate by inheritance, will, distribution of matrimonial assets, expropriation or otherwise not by conveyance.'

provisions of the Code of Real Estate. Instead, general principles of contract law were applied, and the buyers were found to have given up their right to additional claims based on a binding contract.

115. Form requirements also apply to a power of attorney for a sale of real estate (Chapter 2, section 3 of the Code of Real Estate) and for a pre-contract on an intended sale of real estate (Chapter 2, section 7 of the Code of Real Estate).

116. Based on Chapter 2, section 3, a power of attorney for such a sale 'shall be in writing', be signed by the seller, and must also include specifications, since it 'shall indicate the attorney and the real estate to be sold'.

117. Based on Chapter 2, section 7(2), a pre-contract is to be concluded in accordance with sections 1 and 3. In addition, 'also the other provisions on the sale of real estate apply to a pre-contract, where applicable'. The said provision moreover states that a pre-contract must 'indicate the deadline for the conclusion of the sale of real estate and the conditions whose fulfilment triggers the sale'. Nevertheless, this provision allows that essential questions like the price and other considerations may be agreed upon at a later stage, on the basis referred to in the pre-contract.

118. The concept of a pre-contract on an intended sale of real estate was addressed in Supreme Court decision KKO 2015:80. The contract under dispute was concluded between a municipality and a company. The object of the contract was a building site and a building that the municipality was to renovate in accordance with the company's requirements. Based on the contract, the company would pay a redemption price for twelve years to the municipality, after which the ownership of the real estate – with a separate deed – would be transferred to the company. The Supreme Court concluded that the contract was, in fact, a pre-contract on an intended sale of real estate. Since the contract had not been formed as required in the Code of Real Estate, it was to be considered null and void.[87]

§10. Sources of the Law of Contracts

119. As was already discussed, the sources of law in Finland have traditionally been sorted into three groups in accordance with their binding effect. According to this categorization, the strongly binding sources of law consist of statutory law or custom in those areas where there is no written law. The supremacy of EU law was also discussed in connection herewith (*see* General Introduction, §3 above).

---

87. Also Supreme Court decision KKO 1993:108 can be observed. The parties had, in connection with a pre-contract on a sale of real estate, agreed on an interest to be paid on the advance payment that would be repaid in case the sale would not become final. A separate contract had been formed on this issue, and the Court did *not* find that it was such a contract that had to be concluded as required in the Code of Real Estate.

120. The lack of complete acts in Finnish contract law leaves room for other sources of law, such as general principles of contract law. However, there has also been a significant growth of legislation in Finnish contract law since the late 1980s.[88]

121. When legislation within the field of contract law is discussed, it is important to observe the separation between mandatory and non-mandatory legislation. Mandatory legislation mainly exists in order to protect a weaker party to a contract, for example, a consumer. Consequently, a mandatory provision hinders the contracting parties from agreeing otherwise on that specific issue to the detriment of the weaker party. A non-mandatory provision does not form an obstacle for the parties' agreement. Consequently, the principle of freedom of contract is still very important in Finnish contract law, especially for B2B contracts.

122. The following, so-called hierarchy of norms, decides the order in accordance with which the norms ought to be applied in a given situation, for instance, when the contracting parties have differing opinions on the meaning of the contract, which thus needs to be interpreted:

(1) mandatory legislation (if any such exists);
(2) the contract between the parties;
(3) a practice, which has been established between the parties and any other usage/custom, which is to be considered binding on the parties;
(4) non-mandatory legislation.[89]

123. Since Finnish contract law overall includes but a few mandatory provisions, the contract between the parties is in reality often the primary source of law. Naturally, this does not mean that the freedom of contract is absolute: also for B2B contracts it is limited by, for example, the principle of reasonableness found in section 36 of the Contracts Act, which was already discussed in short (*see* Introduction to the Law of Contracts, §8 above).

124. Mandatory provisions are, for instance, found in the Consumer Protection Act (38/1978). According to Chapter 5, section 2 of the said act, which deals with the sale of consumer goods (as amended 16/1994), '[a] contract term differing from the provisions of this chapter to the detriment of the buyer shall be void unless otherwise provided below'. In other words, the chapter contains mainly mandatory provisions.

125. The Sale of Goods Act (355/1987) is non-mandatory in full. This is clearly stated in section 3: 'The provisions of this Act are subject to the terms of the contract between the parties, to any practice which has been established between them and to any other usage which is to be considered binding on the parties.'

---

88. Hemmo 2008, 48.
89. Hemmo 2008, 294.

126. Based on the hierarchy of norms, which is also articulated in the reported section 3 of the Sale of Goods Act, a practice established between the parties (on the basis of previous dealings between them) or any other commercial usage/custom should be taken into account if the question at hand cannot be resolved through the application of contract terms – self-evidently provided that no mandatory legislation exists. Generally, a commercial usage needs to be sufficiently widely spread – which normally happens over time when used – and stable in order to be of significance. Certainly, more is also demanded of a usage which is to set aside non-mandatory law compared to one, where no such law exists. A party does not either necessarily have to be aware of the content of existing practice within a specific field in order to be bound by it (consumers excluded): In other words, the ignorant party must take the consequences of its ignorance. A practice may, however, not be against the law or business morality.[90] It may be pointed out that in its decision KKO 2001:34, the Supreme Court stated that the party who invokes the commercial practice or usage in question also has the burden of proof concerning the same.

127. The contractual legislation in Finland consists, to a significant extent, of general clauses and other kinds of open, flexible norms. This naturally leaves room for different possible interpretations. Guidelines for the intended interpretation of a provision, together with examples of typical situations where it is to be applied, can be found in the legislative preparatory work (*travaux préparatoires*). Furthermore, case law – especially precedents from the Supreme Court – clarifies the application of general clauses. However, not nearly all contractual questions have been clarified in (specific enough) legislation or court practice. Thus, general principles of contract law and various 'real arguments' are, in reality, important sources of law.[91]

128. The Nordic legislative cooperation within the field of contract law has traditionally been significant. Consequently, even legal writing and court practice from the other Nordic countries – Sweden in particular – is a noteworthy source of law in Finland. This is the case provided that the relevant legislation is consistent with the Finnish one, and no divergent interpretations have been made in Finland.[92]

129. The fact that Finland is a member of the EU naturally has an impact on the sources of the law of contracts. This is especially concerning specific contract types; for example, the Consumer Protection Act has been amended on several occasions on the basis of EU directives. From the beginning of 2022, the Consumer Protection Act will, for instance, be amended on the basis of Directive (EU) 2019/770 on certain aspects concerning contracts for the supply of digital content and digital services, as well as Directive (EU) 2019/771 on certain aspects concerning contracts for the sale of goods. Certainly, the ongoing harmonization of European contract law/civil law is interesting also for Finland.

---

90. Saarnilehto 2009, 40, Sund-Norrgård 2014, 64–65.
91. Hemmo 2008, 48–49.
92. Hemmo 2008, 49–50.

130. In Spring 2015, I examined whether the DCFR – which perhaps can be characterized as a revised and much more comprehensive version of the PECL – is used as sources of law by the Supreme Courts of Finland and Sweden, respectively. I found that the Finnish Supreme Court, in its decision KKO 2015:26, for the first time made a reference to DCFR in its judgment (in this case to Article IV.B. – 4:104, Remedies to be directed towards the supplier of the goods). In comparison, the first time that the Swedish Supreme Court used DCFR in its work was in decision NJA 2009 page 672. This judgment was given five and half years earlier than the Finnish one, and since then, the Swedish Supreme Court has made references to DCFR on several occasions. In Finland, the situation is different: the Finnish Supreme Court made for the second – and so far last – time a reference to DCFR in its judgment KKO 2018:37 (in this case to Articles IV.E. – 2:302, Contract for an indefinite period, and III. – 1:109, Variation or termination by notice). Perhaps one dares to conclude from this that DCFR is not (at least not yet) an established source of law in Finnish contract law.[93] Certainly, a possible future Common European Sales Law, and perhaps even a European Civil Code, will also be of relevance in Finland.[94]

131. An important international source of law is the CISG, which entered into effect in Finland on 1 January 1989,[95] and certainly the Unidroit Principles on International Commercial Contracts (Unidroit Principles) have significance as well.

---

93. Sund-Norrgård I 2015. *See also* the opinion expressed in Lando 2009, 758, that is that the future will show us, whether PECL and DCFR to any significant extent will have an impact on Nordic law.
94. *See* Sund-Norrgård I 2015, 526 and references for information on these instruments.
95. United Nations Commission on International Trade Law, Status: United Nations Convention on Contracts for the international Sale of Goods, https://uncitral.un.org/en/texts/salegoods/conventions/sale_of_goods/cisg/status.

Part I. General Principles of the Law of Contracts

Chapter 1. Formation

§1. Agreement and Quid Pro Quo (Reciprocity)

I. Offer and Acceptance

132. A contract is, in accordance with the traditional (classical) view, first and foremost a legal act; there is not much focus on interaction and cooperation between people. According to the classical view, a contract is formed when an offer is accepted, and the other ways to conclude contracts are seen as exceptions.

133. The Contracts Act (228/1929) contains general provisions on the conclusion of contracts through offer and acceptance. Chapter 1, section 1(1) states: 'An offer to conclude a contract and the acceptance of such an offer shall bind the offeror and the acceptor as provided for below in this chapter.' However, the Contracts Act does not include any definition of the concept 'offer'. The offer must nonetheless clearly show the offeror's will to be bound by it, and the offer must be detailed enough in order to enable the acceptor to accept it. The offer must also be directed towards a limited enough crowd; offers directed towards unspecified crowds are usually considered non-binding.[96]

134. In Chapter 1, section 1(2) of the Contracts Act, it is made clear that the provisions of the said chapter do not apply to 'contracts of standard form or to contracts which require performance in order to become effective'. Whereas contracts of standard form (in Finnish: *määrämuotoisia sopimuksia*) certainly exist, contracts which require performance in order to become effective nowadays lack importance.[97] The acquisition of real estate is an example of a contract of standard form, the conclusion of which does not fall under the said provisions of the Contracts Act. Provisions on how to conclude such contracts are instead found in the Code of Real Estate (540/1995). Form requirements of the Code of Real Estate were already discussed above (*see* Introduction to the Law of Contracts, §9).

---

96. Hemmo 2008, 78.
97. Hemmo 2008, 74.

135. It should be noted that the provisions of Chapter 1 of the Contracts Act are non-mandatory: Section 1(2) states that they shall not apply 'where the contrary is expressly or implicitly stipulated in the offer or the acceptance or follows from trade usage or other practice'. Thus, although the offer and acceptance model/mechanism for concluding contracts may be helpful as a 'thinking-scheme', it will self-evidently not be sufficient for every situation where contracts are concluded in today's world. A contract may certainly also be considered concluded where no explicit offer and/or acceptance can be found in the interaction between the parties. The offer and acceptance mechanism – which in short is about accepting or reject-ing an offer made – is neither that useful for implicit agreements, detailed contracts formed on the basis of lengthy negotiations, nor for contracts based on standard terms (in Finnish: *vakioehdot*).[98]

136. There is not necessarily any offer or acceptance involved in a situation where a person gets on a bus and is being transported by the driver. The same goes for a situation where the parties cooperate in a 'contractual manner', although one cannot later show when exactly, or how, the contract was concluded. Still, implicit agreements are formed in situations like these. When parties conclude a contract as a result of negotiations, their wish is also normally to discuss/negotiate issues with the option of still withdrawing from the deal. In other words, the offer and accep-tance mechanism is not useful in the negotiation process.

137. Supreme Court decision KKO 2010:23 is an interesting one on contract for-mation that was largely discussed at the time of the ruling. First of all, it is a case about parking surveillance, which always seems to stir up emotions. Further, in this case, one may also have differing opinions on its private and/or public nature.[99] I will nonetheless solely focus on the contractual aspects of this case, which involved parking on private premises equipped with signs according to which only those with a parking permit were allowed to park in the marked parking spaces. The signs included information on the fact that parking contrary to the conditions would result in a surveillance fee of EUR 40, and that 'by parking you accept these conditions'. The question to be answered by the Supreme Court was whether a contract on these conditions had been formed between a person parking his car in this space and the company handling the surveillance of it. In other words, was the driver obliged to pay the fee of EUR 40 since he had parked contrary to the conditions mentioned on the signs? The Supreme Court stated that there are many contracts that are not formed through offer and acceptance and that in those situations, conclusions may be drawn by applying the principles of the Contracts Act to new situations or by objectively analysing the actions of the parties: certain actions in certain situations may thus lead to the conclusion that a contract is formed. The Supreme Court more-over stated that access to paid parking is often handled in such a way that a car can-not leave the premises without paying a fee. In the case at hand, the situation was nevertheless different: one did not have to pay for parking, but parking was, with some exceptions, prohibited, and in case one acted contrary to the prohibition, there

---

98. Hemmo 2008, 73–74, 85.
99. Mäkinen 2011.

was an obligation to pay a fixed surveillance fee. The Supreme Court was of the opinion that this situation was neither surprising nor exceptional from the point of view of the driver: In many places, parking presupposes that one follows different signs. In addition, parking is often subject to a fee, and wrongful parking may lead to a parking fine. A driver must also be aware that parking on private premises without a permit is prohibited. The Supreme Court thus found that since the owner had placed prohibition signs on the premises with information about the surveillance fee, one could conclude that such conditions had been created based on which a person, parking his car contrary to the prohibition, was to be considered contractually liable for paying the surveillance fee. The Supreme Court considered that the driver, due to the clear signs, knew that he had parked his car on private premises, where parking was prohibited, and where actions against the prohibition would lead to an obligation to pay the surveillance fee in question. He was thus instructed to pay the fee.

138. Another interesting question, which nonetheless will not be further elaborated here, is that of the differences between – in principle non-binding – letters of intent (in Finnish: *aiesopimus*), and binding pre-contracts (in Finnish: *esisopimus*), which the parties may conclude during the negotiation process. The nature of the instrument at hand may certainly have an impact on the possibility to withdraw from the deal, etc. These issues were discussed, for example, in Supreme Court decision KKO 1996:7.

139. Concerning contracts that are based on standard terms, it can be noted that in Article II. – 1:109 of DCFR, the concept 'standard term' is defined as 'a term which has been formulated in advance for several transactions involving different parties and which has not been individually negotiated by the parties'. No such definition is found in any laws in Finland. It is not necessarily important either in every given situation to separate individually negotiated terms from standard terms: the existing legal rules are usually applicable to both kinds. In addition, a contract can be composed of both individually negotiated terms and standard terms. Some principles for the interpretation of standard terms have nonetheless been developed.[100]

140. One basic problem with standard terms, which is of interest when contract formation is discussed, is certainly the question of their binding effect. There are various ways in which they may become part of the contract, for instance, as a result of the parties signing a contract document that includes the standard terms. They typically also become part of the contract when a reference to them is made in the individually negotiated contract or in an offer. In such a case, it is generally presupposed that one must have had a real possibility to acquaint oneself with the standard terms before concluding the contract: Issues such as the period of time that has been reserved for this, as well as whether the terms in question are commonly used, will be of relevance in the contemplation.[101]

---

100. Wilhelmsson 2008, 46.
101. Aspects of this kind were discussed also by the Supreme Court in decisions KKO 1993:45, KKO 1997:164, and KKO 2001:126.

141. If a reference to the standard terms is included in the marketing materials and the like, and not in the contract itself, the question of their binding effect becomes more unclear. In addition, it has been concluded that a binding effect can be the result also without a reference to the standard terms; this can follow from a practice which has been established between the parties or from commercial practice/usage within the field in question. Certainly, the binding effect also depends on whether or not the standard terms can be perceived as balanced: the more unbalanced terms, the more is also demanded in order for them to become binding upon the other party. This is especially so in case the other party is a consumer or otherwise is to be considered weaker.[102] Standard terms are also discussed below (*see* Chapter 3, §1, III).

142. Chapter 1 of the Contracts Act on the conclusion of contracts stipulates, for instance, the following concerning the offer and acceptance: If an offer includes a specific period of time for acceptance, the acceptance has to reach the offeror within the said period of time in order for a contract to be formed (section 2(1)). If an offer is made orally, without granting respite for acceptance, it must be accepted immediately (section 3(1)). If an offer is made in a manner (in a letter, etc.) that makes an immediate acceptance impossible in a situation where no specific period of time has been fixed for acceptance, the acceptance must reach the offeror within a period of time that could reasonably be contemplated by him at the time of making the offer (section 3(2)).

143. An acceptance that reaches the offeror too late is considered to constitute a new offer made by the original acceptor, which then may be accepted by the original offeror if he so wishes (section 4(1)). However, this does not apply 'if the acceptor has assumed that the acceptance has reached the offeror within due time and the offeror must have understood the same'. A contract may in these situations be formed on the basis of the offeror's passivity, since an offeror, who does not wish to accept the acceptance, 'shall, without undue delay, notify the acceptor thereof; otherwise a contract shall be deemed concluded by way of the acceptance' (section 4(2)).

144. An offer, which is rejected, expires even if its period of validity has not yet lapsed (section 5). It is moreover made clear in section 6(1) that an acceptance must be 'clean' in order for a contract to be formed. It states: 'A reply that purports to be an acceptance but which, due to an addition, restriction or condition, does not correspond to the offer, shall be deemed a rejection constituting a new offer.' However, also here, a contract may in certain situations be formed on the basis of the offeror's passivity, since according to section 6(2), this 'shall not apply if the offeree has considered the reply to correspond to the offer and the offeror must have understood the same'. Thus, if the offeror does not wish to accept the reply, he must, 'without undue delay, notify the offeree thereof; otherwise a contract shall be deemed concluded on the terms contained in the reply'.

---

102. Wilhelmsson 2008, 65–84, Saarnilehto 2009, 62–66.

145. An offer or an acceptance can certainly also be revoked and considered not binding. This presupposes that 'the revocation reaches the person to whom it is addressed before, or at the same time as, the offer or acceptance comes to his/her attention' (section 7).

II. Intention to Create Legal Relations

146. A contract has in legal writing been described as a combination of two or more legal/juridical acts, which presume each other.[103] It has also been defined as 'a combination of two or several promises (transactions), through which the parties intentionally seek to a joint goal, with binding effect of the (rights and) obligations thus created, which are also enforceable and recognized by the law'.[104]

147. Certainly, a contract usually is based upon the parties' conscious acts with the intention to be bound by the stipulations of the contract. Nonetheless, the binding effect of a contract always requires neither a clear intention to commit nor an explicit expression of such an intention.[105] A contract can, for instance, be formed as a result of a party's passivity. Issues of this kind were already discussed above (*see* Introduction to the Law of Contracts, §1).

III. Consideration

A. *This Requirement Does Not Exist in Finnish Contract Law*

148. In Finnish contract law, no consideration or similar is required in order for a contract to become legally binding. Thus, Finnish contract law differs from common law in this respect.

B. *Gratuitous Promises*

149. For instance, in English law, a gratuitous promise – that is a promise, which is not supported by consideration (for instance, if you offer to give something without asking for anything in return) – is not generally enforceable.[106] The binding effect of gratuitous promises is recognized in Finnish contract law.

150. According to section 1(1) of the Finnish Gift Promises Act (625/1947), a promise to make a gift concerning goods must be made in writing – in a promissory note or other deed that has been handed over to the recipient of the gift – in order

---

103. Saarnilehto et al. 2012, 309.
104. Toiviainen 2008, 73.
105. Hemmo 2008, 26–27.
106. Hall Ellis Solicitors, Consideration: Contract Law (Meaning, Types & Purpose), https://hallellis.co.uk/contractual-consideration/.

to be considered binding. Such a promise is also binding if it was made in circumstances from which one may conclude that it was intended to become public.

151. Although a promise was made in line with section 1(1), it is, according to section 1(2) of the said act, considered non-binding towards the giver's creditors in case the gift has not been completed.

152. According to section 5(1) of the Finnish Gift Promises Act, it is possible to cancel or lessen a gift after a binding promise has been made but before the gift is completed. This is possible where it is to be considered manifestly unjust to require completion of the gift owing to the fact that the giver's financial situation has considerably deteriorated. In this contemplation, the receiver's situation is to be taken into consideration as well.

153. In case the receiver commits a wrong towards the giver of the promise, the gift may, in accordance with section 5(2) of the said act, be cancelled before it is completed. However, the receiver must be informed of the cancellation within one year from when the giver of the promise became aware of the wrongdoing.

154. The Finnish Gift Promises Act moreover includes provisions on when a gift is to be considered completed. For instance, if someone with the intention to donate in another's name has deposited money, securities or other goods in a credit institution or similar, without retaining the right to dispose of the deposition, the gift is considered completed when the said credit institution has received the goods on behalf of the recipient (section 4, as amended 216/2019).

C. 'Natural Obligations' Do Not Exist in Finnish Contract Law

155. The distinction between civil obligations, which are enforceable by action in a court of law, and natural obligations, 'where the creditor does have a right without a remedy, or at least the traditional remedy',[107] does not exist in Finnish contract law.

IV. Modifications of the Contract

156. Especially for B2B contracts, the assumption is that the parties have had, and have used, their freedom of contract in the contract drafting process. Consequently, once a contract has been concluded, it is considered binding upon the parties (*pacta sunt servanda*). In Saarnilehto's words, the price of freedom of contract is the binding effect of contract.[108]

---

107. Snyder 1966, 423.
108. Saarnilehto 2009, 38.

157. The view, according to which the contract is binding upon the parties in its original form (self-evidently as long as it is not contrary to the law), originates in a traditional (classical) view of contracts, which treats contract parties as enlightened competitors who focus on minimizing risk through adequate clauses included in a non-flexible contract without gaps.[109] This view also means that the parties must jointly agree on modifications to a contract: Normally, unilateral modifications are not considered to be in line with *pacta sunt servanda*. In other words, a party unsatisfied with the contract is not to be given the right to alter the mutually agreed upon rights and duties and risk allocation to the detriment of the other party. This is certainly a logical starting point: what would otherwise be the point with contracts (from a legal point of view)? Moreover, if the party wishing to alter the contract is the stronger party, the principle of *pacta sunt servanda* will, in situations like these, protect the weaker party.[110] This is certainly a good reason not to freely allow modifications.

158. A classical view of contracts, focusing on predictability and allocation of risk (instead of inter-party cooperation), is strengthened when contracts include merger clauses (integration clauses) and written modification clauses. According to the merger clause, the written contract contains the whole agreement between the parties on the issue at hand. Thus, it is used in order to avoid that pre-contractual negotiations, and the like will impact the interpretation of the contract. A written modifications clause demands that modifications ought to be in writing in order to become valid. Thus, the clause is used in order to avoid the parties' oral statements, etc. after the conclusion of the contract, will have an impact on how the contract is interpreted.[111]

159. Based on the principle of freedom of contract, it is possible to include a clause on the right to unilateral modifications in the contract. If the contract does *not* include such a clause, unilateral modifications are, as a starting point, seldom considered acceptable.[112] For instance, in Supreme Court decision KKO 1992:50, a bank was not allowed to unilaterally increase the interest rate of a housing loan it had issued to A. The bank had in the past given a picture of these kinds of loans that they were bound to the Bank of Finland's base rate and would thus change only if the base rate changed. This had been the common understanding of these loans, as well as A's understanding of this particular loan, which the Supreme Court found that the bank must have been aware of. The terms of the loan were not in conflict with A's understanding, and the terms did not include an express right for the bank to unilaterally increase the interest rate. The bank could not either show that it, during the loan negotiations or at signing, had clearly informed A of other possibilities to increase the interest rate.

---

109. Sund-Norrgård 2011, 41 and references.
110. Hemmo 2008, 358.
111. The impact and interpretation of these clauses is discussed further in, for example, Norros 2008, 196–207. *See also* Sund-Norrgård 2011, 178–181.
112. Hemmo 2008, 357–358.

160. It can also be noted that in decision KKO 2016:10, the Supreme Court stated that a contract clause that allows a party to a contract to unilaterally modify essential rights and duties – such as the agreed upon risk allocation – is to be interpreted narrowly.[113]

161. It is more often considered justifiable to allow for 'technicalities' to be unilaterally modified compared to such modifications of clauses, which are perceived as 'essential' from the point of view of the contractual balance agreed upon between the parties. Clauses on a right to unilateral modifications are also usually more acceptable if they are somehow limited – maybe they give the right to modify only certain contract clauses – as opposed to being unlimited by nature.[114]

162. Another variation is to include the exact mechanism for a specific contract modification in the (original) contract. Thus, in such a case, the parties have already in the contract agreed upon how its content will be affected by a certain upcoming event. An index clause that allows changes in the charge in case the grounds for calculation change can be mentioned as an example. In comparison to unlimited unilateral modifications clauses, such clauses are often more exact and clear. For this reason, they are not as likely to be considered unfair.[115]

163. Despite the rather traditional views expressed here, it should be stressed that the general Nordic contract law of today in fact is more correctly described as relatively modern than very traditional. The principle of *pacta sunt servanda* is not as fundamental as it used to be, and contracts are not necessarily seen as instruments for risk allocation only; it is widely recognized that contracts may be long-term relations where terms may, or even are likely to, change as the relation evolves. For instance, based on the so-called proactive contracting approach, an '*ex ante-*take' on contracts is preferred: it is about planning in advance, discussing and cooperating, and concluding contracts that actually work for the parties, thus avoiding unnecessary conflicts.[116] In the case of a long-term cooperation based on trust, it may work well to conclude a flexible, shorter contract that might even include conscious gaps (in order to keep the costs down during negotiations, etc.). The parties are thus more focused on reaching a common goal as smoothly as possible than on risk allocation, and it is natural to also discuss and renegotiate the clauses during the contract term.[117]

---

113. *See also* Hemmo 2008, 342–343.
114. Hemmo 2008, 357, 359–360.
115. Hemmo 2008, 361.
116. *See*, for instance, the discussion in Sund-Norrgård 2011, 98–100, and Haapio 2013, 30–45.
117. Sund-Norrgård 2011, 100–103, Sund-Norrgård et al. 2015.

164. From a more modern take on contracts also follows that at times the principle of loyalty, which has been viewed as a 'counter-principle' to freedom of contract,[118] may lead to modifications of the contract: It may thus be perceived as disloyal to hold on to every detail agreed upon in the contract in situations where the circumstances have changed.[119]

165. When the binding effect of a contract is to be determined, this modern, more dynamic contract law focuses rather on the content of the contract at that point in time than on the circumstances during which the contract was concluded. In terms of contract modifications in court proceedings this, for instance, means that contract terms that have become unbalanced with time may be adjusted in accordance with the already briefly discussed principle of reasonableness of section 36 of the Contracts Act (*see* Introduction to the Law of Contracts, §1 and §8). Section 36 of the Contracts Act states: 'If a contract term is unfair or its application would lead to an unfair result, the term may be adjusted or set aside.' However, it continues by stating that '[i]n determining what is unfair, regard shall be had to the entire contents of the contract, the positions of the parties, the circumstances prevailing at and after the conclusion of the contract, and to other factors'. Consequently, it is not possible to solely assess the reasonableness of a particular contract clause,[120] and already from the wording of the provision, it is clear that 'the positions of the parties' must be observed. It is a fact that courts fairly seldom adjust contracts that have been concluded between (economically) equal parties.[121] There are, however, no real obstacles to adjusting such contracts,[122] and perhaps the importance of section 36 of the Contracts Act will increase in Nordic contract law in the future; perhaps this will be true also for B2B contracts. At the moment there is, for example, an ongoing discussion on the possibilities to adjust contracts that have become unfair as a result of the COVID-19 pandemic.[123]

166. For B2C contracts, mandatory provisions in the legislation may lead to modifications of such contract terms that deviate from the legislation to the detriment of the weaker party.[124]

167. Sometimes, the right to unilateral modifications is found in the legislation itself. For instance, according to section 18 of the Act on Combined Travel Services (901/2017), the organizer may in the contract terms reserve the right to increase the price of the travel after the conclusion of the contract provided that the organizer at

---

118. Mäenpää 2010, 327 and references.
119. Sund-Norrgård 2011, 43.
120. Supreme Court decisions KKO 2001:27 and KKO 2010:9, Wilhelmsson 2008, 119.
121. Government bill 247/1981, 3, 14–15, Hemmo II 2003, 64–66, Wilhelmsson 2008, 122–124, Saarnilehto et al. 2012, 110–111, Sund-Norrgård 2014, 103–108.
122. Grönfors & Dotevall 2016, 259–260.
123. Lindskog 2015, 327, Gomard et al. 2015, 178, and Hoppu 2020.
124. *See* Ch. 4 of the Consumer Protection Act (38/1978, as amended 1259/1994) for provisions applicable to unreasonable terms in B2C contracts. Also Ch. 10, s. 2 of the Employment Contracts Act (55/2001) can be observed; it concerns unreasonable terms in employment contracts.

the same time undertakes to lower the price for a corresponding reason. The acceptable grounds for price changes are for instance changes in the cost of transport that are dependent upon fuel prices, tax changes that affect travel services and exchange rate movements affecting the cost of travel. The price may not be increased during the twenty days preceding the travel.

168. Also, Chapter 7, section 11 of the Employment Contracts Act (55/2001) can be mentioned in connection herewith. The provision gives the employer the right 'to change the employment relationship unilaterally into a part-time relationship on the termination grounds referred to in section 3, and observing the period of notice'. Section 3 refers to financial and production-related grounds for termination.

169. Certainly, the employees' general obligation in Chapter 3, section 1 of the said act to 'perform their work carefully, observing the instructions concerning performance issued by the employer within its competence' is worth mentioning too. The line between the employer's right to give instructions and contract modifications is not necessarily an easy one to draw. It, for instance, seems to be rather clear on the basis of case law that the employer usually has the right to instruct the employee to temporarily do such work that is directly connected to his normal work and thus does not essentially change the quality of the work. This does not change the fact that the self-evident starting point also for employment contracts is *pacta sunt servanda*, and there is no general provision in the Employment Contracts Act on the parties' right to unilateral contract modifications. The question of the employer's right to unilateral modifications – which usually is at least not allowed for essential contract clauses – has nevertheless been largely discussed in legal writing and case law.[125] It will not be addressed further in this monograph.

§2. FORMAL AND EVIDENTIAL REQUIREMENTS

I. Formal Requirements

A. *Contracts under Seal Do Not Exist in Finnish Contract Law*

170. Contracts under seal, that is, contracts that are conclusive when 'signed, sealed, and delivered', do not exist in Finnish contract law.

B. *'Solemn' Contracts Do Not Exist in Finnish Contract Law*

171. Solemn contracts do not exist in Finnish contract law, but form requirements that (perhaps) functionally correspond to the said concept do exist for certain contract types. For instance, according to Chapter 2, section 1 of the Code of Real Estate (540/1995), '[a] sale of real estate shall be concluded in writing. The seller

---

125. An overview is presented in, for example, Tiitinen & Kröger 2012, 814–832.

and the buyer or their attorneys shall sign the deed of sale. A notary shall attest the sale in the presence of all the signatories of the deed of sale'. Due to amendment 96/2011 to the Code of Real Estate, it is, however, nowadays also possible to conclude sales of real estate electronically.

II. Evidential Requirement: Proof

A. The Parol Evidence Rule Does Not Exist in Finnish Contract Law

172. Finnish contract law does not include a parol evidence rule or similar, according to which the contract interpretation is solely focused on the (four corners of the) contract. On the contrary, for instance, the Supreme Court stated in its decision KKO 2001:34 that not solely the wording of the contract is decisive in the interpretation. One must also take into consideration all other materials that impact the content of the contract, such as the negotiations that preceded the contract formation.[126] Having said this, other materials than the written contract document are in practice not always observed in the Nordic countries either. So, despite the fact that the contract law certainly renders it possible to take all relevant aspects into consideration when interpreting a contract, the written contract may nonetheless become decisive, for example, in court proceedings.[127]

B. Function of the Notary

173. The notary services of the Digital and Population Data Services Agency handle the notarizations of signatures and copies of certificates, as well as the authentication of resumes. The services can also confirm a person's rights to act on behalf of a company or public authority, etc. Moreover, the public notary provides services such as purveying protestations of bills, opening and closing safe-deposit boxes and overseeing lotteries.[128]

174. The notary public (or public notary) is regulated in the Act on Notary Public (420/2014, as amended 1150/2019), according to which the director general at the Digital and Population Data Services Agency appoints the officials that become public notaries. It is demanded by law that the person working as a notary public has completed another high academic degree in law than a master's in international and comparative law.[129]

175. It can be especially noted that the notary public handles the type of certification called *apostille* that will legalize documents for use in other countries. This

---

126. *See also* Supreme Court decision KKO 1990:99.
127. Sund-Norrgård 2011, 23 and references.
128. Digital and Population Data Services Agency, https://dvv.fi/en/services-of-notary-public, section 2 of the Act on Notary Public.
129. Section 1 of the Act on Notary Public.

certification relates to official documents and certificates provided by authorities and is necessary if the documentation in question is to be presented to the authority of a country that has ratified the Hague Convention (Convention de La Haye du 5 Octobre 1961).

176. Public notaries are qualified to do their work throughout Finland. A certificate by the notary public is to be confirmed with a stamp, a seal or in a correspondingly reliable manner.[130]

177. There is a separate Act on Public Purchase Witnesses (573/2009). Based on section 3 of the said act, public purchase witnesses authenticate sales of real estate, which is demanded in the Code of Real Estate (540/1995). Notary publics are qualified to be public purchase witnesses, but there are also other instances than notary publics that can act as public purchase witnesses.[131]

III. Burden of Proof

178. As a starting point, the burden of proof in a civil case rests with the party who asserts a legally relevant circumstance. This is made clear in Chapter 17 of the Code of Judicial Procedure (4/1734, as amended 732/2015). Section 2(1) of the said chapter states: 'In a civil case, the party shall prove the circumstances on which his or her claim or objection is based.' According to section 2(2), '[a] circumstance may be taken as grounds for the judgment only on the condition that a party has presented credible evidence regarding it'.[132] Consequently, a party claiming that a contract has, in fact, been concluded usually has the burden of proof for this claim.[133] When a contract is proven, but the parties differ in its content, the contract must be interpreted. The aim of contract interpretation, where the contract between the parties in reality often is the primary source of law, is to establish the common purpose of the contract/common intention of the parties. The sources to be used in contract interpretation were already discussed above (*see* Introduction to the Law of Contracts, §10). In connection herewith, the so-called hierarchy of norms was explained as well.

179. Even though contract interpretation will be discussed also below, it can be noted already here that the starting point in the interpretation of a contract concluded between equal parties is the wording of the contract. This is logical since one

---

130. Sections 3 and 4 of the Act on Notary Public.
131. Section 1 of the Act on Public Purchase Witnesses (as amended 318/2014 and 1143/2019). *See also* the information found at National Land Survey of Finland, Public Purchase Witnessing, https://www.maanmittauslaitos.fi/en/apartments-and-real-property/real-property-and-property-transactions/public-purchase-witnessing.
132. Chapter 17, s. 2(4) of the Code of Judicial Procedure shows that exceptions exist. It states: 'The provisions of subsections 1 and 2 apply unless provisions elsewhere in law provide otherwise regarding the burden of proof or the strength of evidence required, or unless the nature of the case requires otherwise.'
133. *See*, for instance, Vuorijoki 1999.

must be allowed to assume that the well-informed, equal parties have been able to draft a contract that corresponds to their common intention. From this follows that the party claiming that the contract does *not* correspond to such common intention usually has the burden of proof for such a claim.[134] It can be noted that it is considered possible for parties to agree in their contract on the division of the burden of proof.[135]

180. In the (objective) interpretation process focusing on the wording of the contract, an expression/term in the contract is usually to be given the meaning that corresponds to its 'normal' meaning in accordance with common language usage. Sometimes, for instance, when a term is 'technical' or 'legal' by nature, its meaning in accordance with the common usage within that field will nonetheless prevail. A term that is used in different contexts in a contract is also normally to be given the same meaning in every context. Such a meaning should 'fit the objectives' of the contract. It can be specifically noted that wrong use of a term will not decide the content of the contract (*falsa demonstratio non nocet*).[136]

181. If one of the contract parties is responsible for an unclear term – for instance, due to the fact that the party in question has drafted the contract alone, or the contract is based on standard terms provided by that party – it is an established principle to interpret the term to the detriment of its drafter (*in dubio contra stipulatorem*). This principle was referred to by the Supreme Court, for example, in decisions KKO 2008:53, KKO 2010:69 and KKO 2016:10.[137]

182. In terms of contractual liability for damages, the reversed burden of proof is the norm. This was already discussed above (*see* Introduction to the Law of Contracts, §4). In other words, although negligence (culpa) is the basis for liability, the existence of a breach of contract in itself indicates that the party in breach has acted negligently. In order to be free from liability, he must thus prove that he has acted diligently or that he is not responsible for the event causing the loss.[138] Also, other existing possibilities were discussed in more detail in connection herewith. For this reason, this issue will not be further enlightened here.

A. *The Distinction Made Between 'Obligation of Means' and 'Obligation of Result'*

183. The distinction between 'obligation of means' and 'obligation of result' is a familiar one in Finnish law. However, the concepts of best efforts, best endeavours, or the like do not as such exist in Finnish contract law.[139] Such clauses are

---

134. Saarnilehto 2009, 149.
135. Virtanen 2005, 486 and references.
136. Hemmo I 2003, 607–624.
137. *See also* the discussion in Sund-Norrgård 2014, 114–117 and references.
138. Mononen 2004, 1389.
139. The concept of best efforts is discussed in Sund-Norrgård 2011, 161–167.

nevertheless sometimes included in contracts.[140] No obligation to act in accordance with best efforts is found in PECL or in DCFR either. Article 5.1.4 of Unidroit Principles, however, differentiates clearly between a duty to achieve a specific result and a duty of best efforts. The said article states: '(1) To the extent that an obligation of a party involves a duty to achieve a specific result, that party is bound to achieve that result. (2) To the extent that an obligation of a party involves a duty of best efforts in the performance of an activity, that party is bound to make such efforts as would be made by a reasonable person of the same kind in the same circumstances.'

184. Generally, 'obligations of means' and 'obligations of result' are included in the same contract, and according to the comments to Article 5.1.4 of Unidroit Principles, the degree of diligence required of a party in the performance varies considerably between these two types of obligations.[141]

185. The obligation of result will usually demand more of the debtor in the sense that if failing to reach a specific result, he cannot waive all sanctions by simply referring to 'doing all he could'. If the debtor has committed to an 'obligation of means', it will be enough if he has acted diligently independently of whether or not the result was reached. The distinction between these two types of obligations can be seen as a form of result-related risk allocation: The creditor will, in fact, bear the risk of reaching the intended result in case the debtor has committed (only) to an 'obligation of means'.[142]

186. In determining the extent to which an obligation of a party involves a duty of (merely) best efforts in the performance of an activity or a duty to achieve a specific result, Article 5.1.5 of Unidroit Principles should be noted. It contains the following open list of factors to be regarded in connection herewith: '(a) the way in which the obligation is expressed in the contract; (b) the contractual price and other terms of the contract; (c) the degree of risk normally involved in achieving the expected result; (d) the ability of the other party to influence the performance of the obligation'. Although Unidroit Principles is not considered a binding source of law, these criteria have value as a frame of reference also in Finland.[143]

---

140. *See* Sund-Norrgård 2011, 166–167 for information on this issue concerning licensing agreements.
141. Unidroit Principles of International Commercial Contracts 2016, https://www.unidroit.org/wp-content/uploads/2021/06/Unidroit-Principles-2016-English-bl.pdf.
142. Norros I 2012, 80–82.
143. This is briefly discussed in, for example, Norros I 2012, 83–84.

§3. LIABILITY AND NEGOTIATIONS

I. Pre-contractual Liability

187. In a discussion on pre-contractual liability, the duty to inform is essential. Namely, the principle of loyalty, which was already discussed above (*see* Introduction to the Law of Contracts, §8), often imposes a duty to inform the other party. This is so not only during the agreement period but also in the pre-contractual phase, where the information duty can be considered especially extensive if the parties are about to conclude a long-term contract based on trust.[144]

188. The content of the duty to inform is unclear and must be decided case by case. It may include objective facts (that are relevant from the point of view of the other party) but not subjective assumptions or the like. The duty to inform can be seen as more extensive in situations where the parties are unequal. However, also a weaker party is obliged to inform the stronger party.[145]

189. The duty to inform is connected with the duty to investigate. Consequently, a party failing to obtain enough information in a situation where he has a duty to do so bears the risk of failure. Since a contract is a cooperation, one should nevertheless not put *too* much emphasis on a party's investigation duty.[146]

190. At least to some extent, a party must also be allowed to take advantage of his position and knowledge. Consequently, if there has been lots of efforts and costs involved in obtaining certain information, it would not be fair to make that party give it up for free. There is usually no duty to inform the other party in situations where both parties have had equal opportunities to obtain the information in question.[147]

191. A pre-contractual information duty may be based on an act. In the Sale of Goods Act (355/1987), for instance, there are many such sections. Section 18(1) is one example which shows the importance of correct pre-contractual information. Namely, based on this section, goods are considered defective 'if they do not conform with information relating to their properties or use which was given by the seller when marketing the goods or otherwise before the conclusion of the contract and the information can be presumed to have had an effect on the contract'.

192. It is noteworthy that according to section 19 of the Sale of Goods Act, the goods shall, despite being sold subject to an 'as is' clause or a similar reservation concerning quality, be considered defective if 'the seller has, before the conclusion of the contract, failed to disclose to the buyer facts relating to the properties or the

---

144. Sund-Norrgård 2011, 85 and references.
145. Vihma 1945, 47–48, Ollila 2016, 939, Supreme Court decisions KKO 1993:130, KKO 2007:72, KKO 2008:91.
146. Taxell 1977, 150–151.
147. Sund-Norrgård 2011, 88 and references.

use of the goods which the seller could not have been unaware of and which the buyer reasonably could expect to be informed about'. An additional requirement is that 'the failure to disclose the facts can be presumed to have had an effect on the contract'.[148]

193. When discussing the pre-contractual information duty, section 33 of the Contracts Act on 'honour and good faith' or business ethics[149] is to be noted as well. This section, which was addressed already above (*see* Introduction to the Law of Contracts, §8) states: 'A transaction that would otherwise be binding shall not be enforceable if it was entered into under circumstances that would make it incompatible with honour and good faith for anyone knowing of those circumstances to invoke the transaction and the person to whom the transaction was directed must be presumed to have known of the circumstances.' Government bill 241/2006 describes section 33 of the Contracts Act as an expression of a general principle of loyalty. The section is considered to safeguard a party's good faith and promote openness since it obliges a party to share such essential and relevant information that the other party lacks knowledge of. In other words, although acknowledging that the starting point is that the parties themselves are to obtain the relevant information, the Government bill also points out the duty of the parties to make sure that there is no information asymmetry between them. Section 33 of the Contracts Act, which invalidates a contract and is thus discussed also below in connection with the conditions of substantive validity (*see* Chapter 2, §2, I), is nonetheless fairly seldom applied in Finnish courts.[150]

II. Breakdown of Negotiations

194. The purpose of contract negotiations is to find out whether it is possible for the parties to conclude a binding contract. To render possible discussing and agreeing on the content of the said contract, the parties must have freedom of negotiation, in other words, a right to withdraw from the negotiation process at any time for any reason. Consequently, there are always some risks involved when deciding to negotiate: in case the negotiations are broken off, each party must, as a starting point, bear its own costs originating in the negotiation process.[151]

195. Even though it is usually allowed to simultaneously negotiate with more than one party,[152] a party is neither entitled to initiate nor continue contract negotiations in case he is not genuinely striving towards concluding a contract.[153] Such a pre-contractual duty of loyalty exists irrespective of whether or not a contract is

---

148. This is pointed out also in DCFR 2009 Volume 1, 498.
149. Sisula-Tulokas 2005, 324, 326.
150. *See*, for example, Sund-Norrgård 2016, 575–478 and references for additional information. *See also* Supreme Court decision KKO 2000:121.
151. Ollila 2016, 934 and references.
152. Ollila 2016, 943.
153. von Hertzen 1983, 229–230, Mähönen II 2000, 135–136, Ollila 2016, 942. This is consistent with Art. 2:301(3) of PECL and Art. 3:301(4) of DCFR as well.

concluded down the line.[154] In other words, although breaking off negotiations that have been conducted in good faith is allowed,[155] contract negotiations may, in certain situations, generate obligations towards the other party or a duty to pay damages to the other party. The Supreme Court stated in its decision KKO 2011:6 that this is especially so if one of the parties, through his conduct, has given the other party reason to believe that a contract will, in fact, be concluded. If, in such a situation, the party expecting conclusion of a contract has started contract preparations or has taken other measures, an unfounded withdrawal from the negotiation process may lead to a duty to pay damages based on culpa in contrahendo (in Finnish: *sopimuksentekorikkomus*). Liability based on negotiations thus requires negligence or intent.[156]

196. According to Ollila, a 'negotiation contract' (in Finnish: *neuvottelusopimus*) must, in order to be considered binding upon the parties, be detailed enough: As a starting point, the content will to a large extent influence whether the (written or oral) negotiation contract is considered to be a letter of intent, which as a rule is non-binding, or a binding pre-contract. The length of the negotiations, the actions of the parties and their will to commit will be of relevance when contemplating the situation at hand; in Ollila's opinion, the parties can certainly be bound by the contract – in other words, obliged to continue the negotiations – already before the contract negotiations have reached their final stages.[157] This can be further illustrated by Supreme Court decision KKO 2009:45, where a limited liability company, after having negotiated a lease of business premises with the owner of the said premises for almost a year, had withdrawn from the negotiation process. Due to the fact that the company had acted in such a way that the owner of the premises had had reason to believe that a lease agreement would, in fact, be formed, the company was obliged to compensate the owner for the income from rents that he had lost, due to the fact that he had declined to continue an existing lease agreement in the belief that a new lease agreement would be concluded with the company. The company was, moreover, instructed to pay for such repairs of the premises that it had required before breaking off the negotiations.

197. In these cases, the other party is normally to be compensated in accordance with the so-called negative interest (in Finnish: *negatiivinen sopimusetu*), which puts him in a financial situation equivalent to the one he would have been in had he not taken part in any contract negotiations. This is different from breaches of contract, where the other party usually is to be compensated in accordance with the so-called positive interest (in Finnish: *positiivinen sopimusetu*). Thus, in the latter

---

154. Sund-Norrgård 2011, 85 and references.
155. von Hertzen 1983, 323–324, Mähönen I 2000, 10.
156. Ollila 2016, 949–950.
157. Ollila 2016, 945.

cases, the compensation is to correspond to the situation where the contract has been fulfilled properly (*see* the discussion in Introduction to the Law of Contracts, §4 above).[158]

---

158. Ollila 2016, 951. *See also* Supreme Court decision KKO 1999:48, where the compensation was in fact based on the positive interest due to 'special causes', such as a law-based duty to conclude a contract with the party offering the most favourable terms.

Chapter 2. Conditions of Substantive Validity

§1. CAPACITY OF THE PARTIES

198. For the existence of legal capacity (in Finnish: *oikeuskelpoisuus*) of a juridical person, registration is crucial; the juridical person does not exist before that point in time. Contract-based obligations may nevertheless fall on those natural persons who acted on behalf of the community lacking legal capacity.[159] Reference can, for instance, be made here to the Limited Liability Companies Act (624/2006). According to Chapter 2, section 9, '[t]he company shall be established upon registration'. Based on Chapter 2 section 10, '[m]easures taken on the behalf of the company before registration shall be at the joint and several liability of the persons deciding on the measures and the persons participating in them'.[160] Also, Chapter 6, section 28 of the said act is to be noted. It deals with situations where a contract may be invalid due to the fact that it is entered into by a representative who lacks the competence to take such measures on behalf of the company. However, situations of this kind will not be further elaborated here.

199. The legal capacity that any natural person in Finland, as a starting point, has – and needs – in order to be able to conclude a binding contract, can be impacted in such a way that the person, in the end, turns out to lack a sufficient degree of legal competence (in Finnish: *oikeustoimikelpoisuus*).[161] This may follow from incompetency, which is at hand when the person concluding a contract is a minor, or an adult, who has been found incompetent: According to section 2 of the Guardianship Services Act (442/1999) 'an incompetent person is defined as a person under 18 years of age (minor) or a person who has attained the age of 18 years (adult) but who has been declared incompetent'. Based on section 3, the affairs of an incompetent person are to be managed by a guardian.

200. In accordance with section 4 of the Guardianship Services Act, a guardian may be appointed for a person who is not incompetent if the person needs support in managing his affairs. Namely, the lack of legal competence can also stem from the fact that the competence of a person has been restricted by court order in accordance with section 18. From this may follow that a person is able to enter into given transactions or administer given property only in conjunction with the guardian, or that he is not competent to enter into given transactions or to administer given property. It is to be noted that only as a 'last resort' will the person be declared (totally) incompetent. Also, otherwise is the competency of a person not to be restricted more than what is necessary for the safeguarding of the interests of that person.

---

159. Hemmo 2008, 189, 196.
160. Nonetheless, obligations arising from measures taken after the signing of the Memorandum of Association that are taken no earlier than one year before the signing shall, in accordance with Ch. 2 s. 9, be transferred to the company.
161. Hemmo 2008, 189.

201. Sections 23–25 of the Guardianship Services Act give an incompetent person the right to 'enter into transactions which, in view of the circumstances, are usual and of little significance'. The person in question also has the right to decide on the proceeds of his own work earned during the incompetency.

202. The Young Workers' Act (998/1993) is to be mentioned in this regard. It applies, based on section 1, to work done by a person under 18 years of age (young worker). According to section 3(1) (as amended 57/2001), '[a] person aged fifteen or more may, as a worker, make a contract of employment himself or give notice on it or cancel it. For a person under 15, a guardian can make the contract of employment or, with the consent of the guardian, it can be made by the young person himself'. Section 3(2) should be observed too. It states: 'The person having care and control of a young worker shall have a right to rescind his contract of employment if this is necessary for the sake of the young worker's education, development or health.'[162]

203. As a starting point, a transaction beyond the competency of an incompetent person is not binding on him. It is a ground for invalidity that is taken into consideration ex officio by courts and other authorities.[163] However, it can still be remedied: Based on section 26 of the Guardianship Services Act, such a transaction shall become binding if the guardian or, after the end of incompetency, the person himself ratifies it.

204. Insolvency – in other words that 'the debtor is otherwise than temporarily unable to repay his or her debts as they fall due' – is relevant for the right to form binding contracts: An insolvent debtor may, based on Chapter 2, section 1 of the Bankruptcy Act (120/2004), be declared bankrupt. A legal consequence of the beginning of bankruptcy is, according to Chapter 3, section 1 of the said act, that 'the debtor shall lose his or her authority over the assets of the bankruptcy estate'. As the main rule, according to Chapter 3, section 2 of the Bankruptcy Act, '[a] transaction entered into by the debtor concerning assets of the bankruptcy estate shall not be binding on the estate'.

---

162. Chapter 1, s. 6 of the Employment Contracts Act (55/2001) can also be noted here. It states: 'Provisions concerning the right of a person under 18 years of age to conclude a contract of employment and the right of the person having the care and custody of a young employee to cancel a contract of employment concluded by a minor are laid down in the Young Workers' Act (998/1993).' It also states: 'A person who has been declared legally incompetent or whose competence has been limited under the Guardianship Services Act (442/1999) may conclude and terminate a contract of employment on his own behalf.'
163. Hemmo 2008, 175.

§2. Defects of Consent

I. Mistake

205. In a discussion on mistake section 32 of the Contracts Act (228/1929) is relevant. Section 32(1) regulates mistakes in the form of misprints or other errors in an expression/declaration made by the person himself. It states: 'Where a message containing an expression of a person's will, due to a misprint or other error on his/her part, differs from what he/she intended, the message shall not bind him/her if the recipient knew or should have known of the misprint or error.'

206. Section 32(2) regulates errors in transmission or mistakes made by a messenger in an originally properly formed expression while delivering the expression. It states: 'Where a message containing an expression of a person's will is transmitted by telegram or orally through a messenger and it changes due to an error in transmission or a mistake made in its delivery by the messenger, the message shall not bind the sender in the form in which it reached the other party even if the recipient was in good faith. After learning of the change the sender shall, however, inform the recipient without undue delay that he/she does not want to be bound by the changed message; otherwise, and provided that the recipient was in good faith, the message shall be binding in the form it reached the recipient.' In other words, the ground for invalidity based on section 32 of the Contracts Act is focused on errors somehow related to the contents of an expression/declaration of a will. It is moreover to be stressed that a bona fide recipient of an erroneous expression of a will is protected on the basis of section 32(1). In a case that falls under section 32(2), the good faith of the recipient is irrelevant provided that the mistaken party, without delay after noticing the error, informs the recipient thereof.[164]

207. Traditional Finnish legal writing distinguishes between a mistake in the expression/declaration of a will, a mistake in the delivery of an expression of a will and a mistake in the motive of expressing a will,[165] or simply between a mistake in the expression/declaration of a will and a mistake in the motive of expressing a will.[166] It has also been common to distinguish, on the one hand, between a mistake in the expression and a mistake in the motive and, on the other, between a mistake of facts and a mistake of law.[167]

208. In case of a mistake in the expression, the will of the person and the content of the expression are *not* equivalent. In the case of a mistake in the motive, the will corresponds to the expression of the will, but the will has been formed on the basis of false assumptions.[168] Both facts and the law can be the object of a mistake

---

164. It can be noted that also DCFR includes a specific article on mistakes of this kind, namely Art. II. – 7:202 (Inaccuracy in communication may be treated as a mistake).
165. Toiviainen 2008, 133 and references.
166. Ämmälä 1993, 58.
167. That is when a person's understanding of the content of the law does not correspond to the actual law in force, *error iuris nocet*.
168. Ämmälä 1993, 74.

in expression as well as the object of a mistake in motive, albeit a mistake of law is typically to be characterized as a mistake in motive. When contemplating the binding effect of a legal act, the traditional approach has been to give relevance to mistakes in expression and mistakes of facts, but *not* to mistakes in motive and mistakes of law. It has been expressed in legal writing that this view is not nowadays a totally satisfactory one. For instance, as to the traditional principle that a mistake of law is to be without legal consequences in the Finnish legal system, Mäkelä stresses that the weight of this general principle of law, in fact, differs between different fields of law. This is a consequence of an increasing amount of legal rules and a legal system that is becoming more and more complex.[169] It can be specifically observed that in DCFR both the mistake of fact and mistake of law are covered by Article II. – 7:201 (Mistake).[170]

209. Section 32 of the Contracts Act does not deal with mistakes in the motive of expressing a will. There is no other specific provision on these mistakes either, and as a main rule, such *error in motivis* has traditionally not been a ground for invalidity. However, it is not always even possible to make a clear distinction between a mistake in expression and a mistake in motive,[171] and for instance, the general clause in section 33 of the Contracts Act, the purpose of which is to give protection against dishonest business methods,[172] may also be applied in situations of mistakes in motive. This is so provided that the other party presumably knew about the mistake, wherefore it would be contrary to honour and good faith to invoke the contract.[173] As a general remark it can be pointed out that section 33 lost much of its original significance when the general clause in section 36 of the Contracts Act (as amended 956/1982) on the right to adjust unfair contracts was introduced in 1983.

210. Section 33 of the Contracts Act states: 'A transaction that would otherwise be binding shall not be enforceable if it was entered into under circumstances that would make it incompatible with honour and good faith for anyone knowing of those circumstances to invoke the transaction and the person to whom the transaction was directed must be presumed to have known of the circumstances.' Section 33, which thus invalidates a contract, is applicable only in situations where the contract in question clearly differs from what is to be perceived as normal,[174] and it is in fact fairly seldom applied by courts.[175] The position of the other party will nonetheless have an impact here: if he is in a position of dependence comparable to the

---

169. Mäkelä 2009, 95–96, Mäkelä 2010, 8, 156–157, 281–282 and references.
170. *See also* the comments to this article in DCFR 2009 Volume 1, 461, according to which 'the mistake may be about the facts surrounding the contract or the law affecting it'.
171. Ämmälä 1993, 58, 75.
172. Lagberedningens publikationer 1925 No. 2, 64–65.
173. Mäkelä 2010, 153–157.
174. Hemmo I 2003, 372.
175. Decision KKO 2000:121, in which case the buyers of a subdivision/definite section of a property had acted dishonestly towards the sellers, is a rather enlightening example of when the Supreme Court has applied s. 33.

one referred to in section 31 of the Contracts Act (on usury/loan sharking),[176] also the prerequisites of section 33 will be more easily met compared to a situation, where the contract is formed between equal parties, or between parties that are not dependent on each other.[177] The necessary conditions/prerequisites for an application of section 33 are nonetheless fairly difficult to prove.[178] This ground for invalidity is not recognized ex officio, but needs to be invoked by the injured party,[179] and it can be remedied.[180]

211. Provisions, which can be characterized as covering a mistake in motive, are also found, for instance in section 17 of the Sale of Goods Act (355/1987), in Chapter 5, section 12 of the Consumer Protection Act (38/1978, as amended 16/1994) as well as in Chapter 2, section 17 of the Code of Real Estate (540/1995). As Mäkelä points out, all of these provisions on defects protect the buyer's justified expectations on the quality and characteristics of the bought goods/real property.[181]

212. It may be noted that DCFR includes a specific article, namely Article II. – 7:203, on adaptation of contract in case of a mistake. As for provisions in Finnish law, section 36 of the Contracts Act should be observed in connection herewith: This general clause that gives a right to adjust unfair contract terms can certainly be used also in case of mistakes.

213. Finally, one may observe the traditional Scandinavian – perhaps mostly Danish and Swedish – so-called doctrine of failed assumptions (in Finnish: *edelly-tysoppi*, in Swedish: *förutsättningsläran*).[182] It has been seen as a complement to the grounds for invalidity in sections 28–33 of the Contracts Act due to the fact that it increases the possibilities for parties to get out of contracts on the basis of mistakes or changed circumstances. In short – at least according to one version of the doctrine – an assumption becomes legally relevant when (1) there has been an assumption, which has been (2) apparent to the other contract party, and (3) has been relevant enough to have had an impact on the party's will to conclude the contract on the agreed conditions, and (4) it is fair that the other party bears the risk for this defect in assumptions.[183]

---

176. Section 31(1) states: 'If anyone, taking advantage of another's distress, lack of understanding, imprudence or position of dependence on him/her, has acquired or exacted a benefit which is obviously disproportionate to what he/she has given or promised or for which there is to be no consideration, the transaction thus effected shall not bind the party so abused.'
177. Hemmo I 2003, 372.
178. Wilhelmsson 2008, 128.
179. The party guilty of acting contrary to honour and good faith may not invoke this ground for invalidity, but some third parties possibly may. *See* Hemmo 2008, 219.
180. Hemmo 2008, 219.
181. Mäkelä 2010, 158.
182. *See also* DCFR 2009 Volume 1, 464, 486.
183. Ramberg & Ramberg 2016, 211–214.

214. In Finland, the approach to the doctrine of failed assumptions has been rather restrictive.[184] Nevertheless, the Supreme Court has on many occasions mentioned the concept 'assumption' (in Finnish: *edellytys*) in its decisions without applying the doctrine of failed assumptions per se. It is thus clear that the Supreme Court is of the opinion that some assumptions are essential for a binding contract. For example, in decision KKO 2012:1, the Supreme Court stated that each party to a contract, as a starting point, is responsible for his own legal acts and commitments. Consequently, if an assumed fact/matter later turns out to be faulty, this too is something that the party normally bears the risk for since he failed to investigate the grounds for his assumptions thoroughly enough. The Supreme Court nonetheless continued by stating that faulty assumptions can be relevant from the point of view of the binding effect of contract in situations where the assumption in question has been essential and decisive for the conclusion of the contract, and the assumption, as well as its relevance for the conclusion of the contract, has been known to the other party. In addition, it is to be demanded that the party, who based his legal act on the assumption, has acted diligently.[185]

II. Misrepresentation

215. That contracts are voidable due to misrepresentation – which, for instance, has been described as '[a]n untrue statement of fact or law made by Party A (or its agent) to Party B, which induces Party B to enter a contract with Party A thereby causing Party B loss' –[186] is a common law doctrine, where the three varieties of misrepresentation, that is fraudulent, negligent and innocent, are treated slightly differently.[187] The doctrine of misrepresentation does not as such have an equivalent in Finnish contract law, but similar provisions can be found in various acts.

216. Before discussing such provisions, it can be noted that also Article II. – 7:205 of DCFR (Fraud), gives the right to avoid a contract when the other party has induced the conclusion of the contract by fraudulent misrepresentation 'by words or conduct, or fraudulent non-disclosure of any information which good faith or fair dealing, or any pre-contractual information duty, required that party to disclose' (Article II. – 7:205(1)). The article contains information on the criteria of a fraudulent misrepresentation (Article II. – 7:205(2)), as well as on such circumstances that particularly is to be regarded in the determination of whether a party, with regard to good faith or fair dealing, should have disclosed particular information (Article II. – 7:205(3)). In the comments to the said article of DCFR, it is stated as a general policy in a case of fraud that 'there is no reason to protect any interest the fraudulent party may have in upholding the contract; nor is the risk of being deliberately mislead one that a party should be expected to bear'. It is also made clear that it is

---

184. Hemmo 2008, 231, Sund-Norrgård 2011, 231 and references.
185. *See also* Supreme Court decisions KKO 1986 II 111 and KKO 1996:83.
186. Practical Law. A Thomson Reuters Legal Solution, http://uk.practicallaw.com/9-107-6848.
187. For information, *see*, for example, Davies on Contract 2004, 112–122.

irrelevant whether the fraudulent statement is as to facts or law. Sales talk and statements of opinion are not covered by the article.[188]

217. In terms of relevant Finnish provisions in this regard, especially section 30 of the Contracts Act (228/1929) on fraud in the inducement, is to be observed. Section 30, which does not offer any explanation as to what is actually meant by the concept, states: 'A transaction into which a person has been fraudulently induced shall not bind him/her if the person to whom the transaction was directed was himself/herself guilty of such inducement or if he/she knew or ought to have known that the other party was so induced.'

218. As for non-disclosure, which is specifically mentioned in the discussed Article II. – 7:205 of DCFR, it can be noted that section 30 of the Contracts Act is applicable also in situations where a party, in bad faith, fails to reveal information that he should have revealed. Namely, according to court practice – which there is very little of – and legal writing, not only the bad faith presentation of false information to the other party, but also bad faith non-disclosure of relevant information is covered by the provision. Fraud in the inducement is about causing the other party to make an essential mistake, for instance, in such a way that if he had known the facts, he would not have formed the contract in question, at least not on identical terms. Thus, the existence of minor discrepancies and errors in the information that forms the basis for the contract does not lead to the conclusion that there is fraud in the inducement.[189] This ground for invalidity is one that is not recognized ex officio and that can be invoked only by the injured party. It is also one that can be remedied.[190]

219. Fraud in the inducement is not a very important ground for invalidity, which may be a consequence of the fact that the prerequisites for it are (even) harder to prove than the prerequisites for the general clause on honour and good faith in section 33 of the Contracts Act.[191]

III. Improper Pressure

220. Sections 28 and 29 of the Contracts Act (228/1929) on grave duress and coercion respectively are the most relevant provisions in Finnish contract law in a discussion on improper pressure. These sections will therefore be illuminated next.

221. In accordance with section 28(1) of the Contracts Act, '[a] transaction into which a person has been coerced shall not bind him/her if the coercion consisted of

---

188. DCFR 2009 Volume 1, 492–493.
189. Ämmälä 1993, 48–49, Hemmo 2008, 205. *See also* DCFR 2009 Volume 1, 498. It may be of interest to also note the criminal equivalences to fraud in the inducement that are found in Ch. 36 of the Criminal Code (1889/39, as amended 769/1990), namely fraud (s. 1), aggravated fraud (s. 2), and petty fraud (s. 3).
190. Hemmo 2008, 206.
191. *Ibid.*

physical violence or a threat involving imminent danger to life or health (grave duress)'. Section 28(2) on such coercion exercised by a third party states: 'However, if the coercion was exercised by a third person and the person to whom the transaction was directed was in good faith, the coerced party shall, if he/she wants to invoke the said coercion in relation to the other party, without undue delay after the coercion has ceased notify that party thereof at the risk of the transaction otherwise becoming binding.'

222. Section 29 on (the less grave forms of) coercion states: 'A transaction entered into under coercion not constituting grave duress, as referred to in section 28, shall not bind the coerced party if the coercion was exercised by the person to whom the transaction was directed or if this party knew or should have known that the other party was coerced into the transaction.' Grave duress thus presupposes physical violence or threats involving imminent use of physical violence.[192] This is not the case in those situations that fall under section 29 of the Contracts Act. Instead, other kinds of harm are relevant here; maybe the coercion is directed towards honour, freedom or property.[193] It is equally made clear in the comments to Article II. – 7:206(1) of DCFR that coercion under DCFR does not necessarily involve the use of threats (although this is normally the case), and moreover that '[r]elief will not be given unless the threat did influence the threatened party's decision'.[194]

223. Another difference between section 28 and section 29 of the Contracts Act is that the good faith of a party is protected under section 29. In other words, the coerced party can invoke the coercion only against a party to the contract who has exercised the coercion himself or should have known about the coercion. Under section 28, this is not so: even if the grave duress was exercised by a third party and the party to the contract was unaware of it, his good faith is *not* protected. The coerced party is, however, under an obligation to make a notification thereof in

---

192. *See also* Ch. 25, s. 7 of the Criminal Code (39/1889, as amended 578/1995), which states: 'A person who raises a weapon at another or otherwise threatens another with an offence under such circumstances that the person so threatened has justified reason to believe that his or her personal safety or property or that of someone else is in serious danger shall, unless a more severe penalty has been provided elsewhere in law for the act, be sentenced for menace to a fine or to imprisonment for at most two years.'

193. It can be noted that the criminal equivalence to coercion is found in Ch. 25, s. 8 of the Criminal Code (39/1889, as amended 578/1995). It states: 'A person who unlawfully by violence or threat forces another to do, endure or omit to do something shall, unless a more severe penalty has been provided elsewhere in law for the act, be sentenced for coercion to a fine or to imprisonment for at most two years.'

194. DCFR 2009 Volume 1, 500. *See also* DCFR 2009 Volume 1, 502, where it is pointed out that the existence of an alternative, such as 'the party could have found someone else to do the work, or could have obtained an order forcing the other party to do it', suggests that the threat was not real, and relief will therefore not be given in such cases. However, the burden of proof for the existence of an alternative of this kind rests with the party making the threat. This is important, since according to Art. II. – 7:206(2), '[a] threat is not regarded as inducing the contract if in the circumstances the threatened party had a reasonable alternative'.

order not to be bound by the contract.[195] Coercion is not recognized ex officio but needs to be invoked by the injured party. It is moreover a ground for invalidity that can be remedied.[196]

224. The problem with these provisions is perhaps not so much the separation of grave duress from the less grave forms of coercion but the separation of cases that fall under section 29 from those that are not to be treated as coercion at all.[197] As an example of this, Supreme Court decision KKO 1996:90 can be noted. The Supreme Court stated here that it is not coercion, but normal procedure for a creditor to demand payment of a negotiable promissory note (in Finnish: *vekseli*) when it is due, as well as to protest it and seek payment through means of compulsion when it is not paid or when the creditor does not agree on its renewal.

IV. Gross Disparity

225. For a discussion on gross disparity, section 31(1) of the Contracts Act (228/ 1929) on usury (loan sharking) is relevant. It states: 'If anyone, taking advantage of another's distress, lack of understanding, imprudence or position of dependence on him/her, has acquired or exacted a benefit which is obviously disproportionate to what he/she has given or promised or for which there is to be no consideration, the transaction thus effected shall not bind the party so abused.' Also, section 31(2) can be mentioned. According to it, '[t]he same shall apply if a third person was guilty of conduct referred to in paragraph (1) and the person to whom the transaction was directed knew or should have known thereof'.[198]

226. In other words, section 31 of the Contracts Act hinders the binding effect of contract on the basis of lack of judgment. Such lack of judgment is to be created by different kinds of distress (financial or other), lack of understanding, imprudence or position of dependence. The lack of understanding referred to in the section may be long-term or short-term, stemming from old age or shock or the participation in an accident, etc. while imprudence may be the result of being under the influence of alcohol or drugs.[199] The position of dependence refers to dependence created through a personal relationship, for instance, the relationship between a parent and a child, or between spouses, but also between an employer and an employee.[200] The position of dependence does not have to be created by the person taking advantage

---

195. Hemmo 2008, 200, Saarnilehto 2009, 120–121.
196. Hemmo 2008, 204.
197. *See* the discussion in Hemmo 2008, 201–203.
198. It may be of interest to also note the criminal equivalences found in Ch. 36 of the Criminal Code (39/1889), namely usury (s. 6 as amended 845/2009), and aggravated usury (s. 7, as amended 769/ 1990).
199. Supreme Court decisions KKO 1949 II 266, KKO 1950 II 471, Saarnilehto 2009, 124.
200. Supreme Court decision KKO 2003:48, Saarnilehto 2009, 125.

of it; the position only needs to be exploited by him. Nevertheless, it must be consciously used in order for the exploiter to receive a benefit obviously disproportionate to what he himself is giving in return,[201] which may be a rather difficult prerequisite to prove in many a case. This is relevant since also section 31 offers a ground for invalidity that is not recognized ex officio but needs to be invoked by the injured party. It can be remedied.[202]

227.   Consequently, it is important to observe that in all such cases that fall under section 31, section 33 of the Contracts Act is applicable as well (albeit the prerequisites of section 33 are not very easy to prove either). Another, perhaps more easily accessible, possibility is to apply section 36 of the Contracts Act. The application of section 36 may be a better option for the injured party also because in that case the contract, at least as a starting point, will stay in force,[203] but with an adjusted, more balanced content.[204] Both section 33 and section 36 have been discussed above (*see* Introduction to the Law of Contracts, §8, and Part I, Chapter 1, §1, IV and §3, I).

228.   The Supreme Court applied section 31 in decision KKO 2003:48, where an elderly (77 years old) sick wife had given her part of the shares that gave the right to occupy the apartment that was used as the couple's common home to her husband for free. The purchase price indicated in the contract – which also was considerably lower than the real value of the shares – had in fact not been paid at all. The conclusion that the husband had taken advantage of his wife's distress in accordance with section 31 was supported by the fact that she had suffered from depression for years and had largely been dependent upon the help of her husband in her everyday life after also having had a cerebral infarction. On top of this, the facts of the case indicated that the husband had been abusive and bossy towards her.

§3. OTHER CONDITIONS OF VALIDITY

I. Existing and Licit Cause Does Not Exist in Finnish Contract Law

229.   There is no doctrine on the existing and licit cause, in other words, that a contractual obligation must have a cause and that the cause must be licit/legal in Finnish contract law.

---

201. Hemmo 2008, 207, Saarnilehto 2009, 125.
202. Hemmo 2008, 209.
203. It is possible to also declare the whole contract terminated on the basis of s. 36.
204. Hemmo 2008, 207–208.

II. Determined or Determinable, Possible and Licit Objects Do Not Exist in Finnish Contract Law

230. The concepts determined or determinable, possible and licit objects are not used in Finnish contract law.

III. Initial Impossibility

231. There is no specific doctrine on initial impossibility in Finnish contract law. Initial impossibility does not as such preclude the formation of a contract or invalidate a contract; it will normally be dealt with as a matter of non-performance. In other words, it is considered equal to such an impossibility that occurs after the conclusion of the contract.

232. The Finnish approach is thus similar to the one taken in Article II. – 7:102 of DCFR (Initial impossibility or lack of right or authority to dispose of), which states: 'A contract is not invalid, in whole or in part, merely because at the time it is concluded performance of any obligation assumed is impossible, or because a party has no right or authority to dispose of any assets to which the contract relates.'[205] When talking about a party having 'no right or authority to dispose of any assets to which the contract relates' (as stated in the said article of DCFR), it can be pointed out that the goods are, based on section 41 of the Sale of Goods Act (355/1987), considered defected '[i]f the goods are subject to a claim of a third party based on ownership, lien or other property right (third-party claim)'.

233. It can be noted that in Finnish law possession of an object/thing (and registration, where applicable) has the effect that third parties may, as a starting point, trust that the possessor really has the right to dispose of the object in question. In other words, the assumption of third parties created by possession is thus protected.[206]

IV. Illegality and Public Policy

234. Grounds for invalidity that cannot be remedied are, for instance, defects in form in situations where the law requires a particular form to a contract. An example of this is the sale of real estate: The form of deed of sale is regulated in Chapter 2, section 1 of the Code of Real Estate (540/1995, as amended 96/2011).

235. Another example is a contract with a purpose contrary to the law, such as someone taking it upon himself to commit a crime. The same goes for contracts that are contrary to certain special legislation of which section 37 of the Contracts Act

---

205. Reference can also be made here to Art. 4:102 of PECL.
206. Tammi-Salminen 2001, 106–107.

(as amended 956/1982) can serve as an example: 'A term under which property pledged as security for an obligation is forfeited if the obligation is not discharged shall be void.'

236. This is so also for contractual arrangements that are contrary to competition law:[207] The Competition Act (948/2011), for instance, forbids cartels in the following fashion in section 5(1): 'All agreements between undertakings, decisions by associations of undertakings, and concerted practices by undertakings which have as their object the significant prevention, restriction or distortion of competition or which result in a significant prevention, restriction or distortion of competition shall be prohibited.' Agreements, decisions or practices that in particular are to be prohibited are (black)listed in section 5(2), while the exemptions are found in Article 6 of the said act.

237. Contracts on such redistribution of wealth that society wants to prevent are invalid. Illegal gambling is one example of this;[208] organized gambling is a crime based on Chapter 17, section 16(1) of the Criminal Code (39/1889, as amended 563/1998). It states: 'A person who unlawfully arranges gambling or keeps a room or other premises for gambling, or as the proprietor of a hotel or restaurant establishment allows gambling to take place, shall be sentenced for organised gambling to a fine or to imprisonment for at most one year.' It is made clear in section 16(2) that gambling is intended to refer to 'pools, bingo, tote and betting games, money and goods lotteries, casino operations and other similar games and activities where winning is completely or partially dependent on chance or events beyond the control of the participants in the game or activity and where the possible loss is clearly disproportionate to the solvency of at least one of the participants'.

238. Fictitious (sham) contracts, where the content of the contract does not reflect the real intentions of the parties,[209] also belong to the category of grounds for invalidity that cannot be remedied. A sham contract is a contract that seems legit on the surface but which neither party has any intention to fulfil in accordance with its content. Such a contract is typically formed in order to avoid taxes or to injure creditors, and it is considered non-binding also *inter partes*. This ground for invalidity is not considered ex officio,[210] but both parties to the fictitious contract, as well as any third party that is directly affected by it (for instance, an injured creditor) may invoke it.[211]

239. Section 34 of the Contracts Act (228/1929) is to be noted here too. This section, which focuses solely on the position of an assignee, states: 'Where a simulated document has been drawn up and the holder under the document of a claim or other right has assigned the said right, the assignee shall be entitled to enforce the right

---

207. Hemmo 2008, 173–179, 185–188.
208. Hemmo 2008, 239.
209. Saarnilehto 2009, 137.
210. It can be noted that according to Ämmälä 1993, 121 this is an issue, which at times is considered ex officio.
211. Hemmo 2008, 235–238.

if he/she acquired it in good faith.' This is thus an exception from the main rule of succession, which is specifically expressed in section 27 of the Promissory Notes Act (622/1947), according to which an assignee will not get a better position than the assignor had.[212] It states: 'When a non-negotiable promissory note is transferred or assigned, the transferee shall not have a better right against the debtor than the transferor had unless expressly otherwise stipulated.'

240. Contracts with a purpose that is contrary to good practice/moral are to be observed too. Namely, even though activities that are contrary to good practice/ moral are not forbidden by law, they are considered unwanted by society and are thus to be prevented. Consequently, also such contracts are in fact considered invalid and are unenforceable in court. This ground for invalidity cannot be remedied. Prostitution can serve as an example: Prostitution is not in itself an illegal activity in Finland, albeit there are many different provisions in place that restrict the activity. Due to the fact that a contract on the offering of sexual services is considered to be contrary to moral, a person who, for instance, has not received the agreed payment for performed sexual services cannot enforce the contract in court. It is not possible in Finland to enforce a contract according to which a person has committed to remain within a certain faith/religion, stay unmarried or similar.[213]

241. It can also be pointed out here that mandatory legislation supersedes such contract clauses that are contrary to it to the detriment of a weaker party (for instance a consumer, an employee). In other words, this is an effect that can be compared to declaring the contract void in part. It is a ground of invalidity that is considered ex officio.[214]

V. Unenforceable Contracts

242. A valid contract can – as a last resort – be enforced through court proceedings, whereas an invalid contract is unenforceable. Different grounds for invalidity have been discussed above in this chapter and will not be enlightened here again. One should nonetheless observe that most grounds for invalidity must be invoked by a party. Thus, if such a ground is in fact *not* invoked, the invalidity is remedied, and the contract can be enforced despite its original invalidity. In these cases, where one does not know if the contract will become binding in the end, the legal state between the parties can be described as unclear.[215]

243. The enforceability of an additional payment will be addressed in short: Focus is on the situation where the price/consideration in the contract is lower than the sum that the parties have (orally) agreed upon. When compared to the above discussed sham contract, this situation is thus different: the intended transaction is real,

---

212. Saarnilehto 2009, 136.
213. Pro tukipiste, https://protukipiste.fi/ihmiskauppa/tunnista-ihmiskauppa/, Hemmo 2008, 243–244.
214. Hemmo 2008, 177.
215. Hemmo I 2003, 313, 319–320.

albeit with a discrepancy between the price of the contract and the real price. Since the payment clause is usually an essential one in a contract, it is fair to ask whether discrepancies between the price mentioned in that clause and the – perhaps considerably higher – price agreed upon may lead to invalidity of the (whole) contract? In Finland, the answer to this question would be 'no'. This is so even for the sale of real property with its specific stipulations as to form. This is made clear in Chapter 2, section 1(3) of the Code of Real Estate (540/1995, as amended 96/2011), according to which the additional payment is nonetheless unenforceable. It states: 'The sale shall not be binding unless it is concluded as provided in this section. If the seller and the buyer have agreed on a price or other consideration in excess of that taken into the deed of sale, the seller shall not have the right to collect the excess amount.'[216] Moreover, a buyer may not either get the additional payment back on the basis of unjust enrichment.[217]

244. Additional payments of this kind in other cases than sales of real property may, in fact, be enforceable, if not agreed upon in order to avoid paying taxes or the like (which, of course, usually is the reason for using such additional payments).[218] The Supreme Court decision KKO 1993:134 can be mentioned in connection herewith. In this case, only a part of the agreed price for a purchase of shares was included in the contract. During signing, the purchase price mentioned in the contract, as well as another part of the agreed price, had been paid by the buyer. He had also given the seller promissory notes covering the rest of the orally agreed price. The Supreme Court found that since there are no provisions to form for contracts of this kind, and since the buyer was not able to show any reason why he was not bound by the promissory notes, he was instructed to also pay the rest of the agreed purchase price to the seller.

§4. The Consequences of a Defect of Consent or a Lack of Substantive Validity

I. Avoidance of the Contract: Nullity

245. In the Nordic countries there are in fact no general rules on the invalidity of contracts, and already the concept itself is somewhat problematic.[219] A contract may nonetheless – as was already discussed above in this chapter – be declared invalid, in whole or in part, based on shortcomings in connection with the parties to the contract (incompetency, etc.), the way in which the contract was formed (coercion, etc.), or the content of the contract (contrary to the law, etc.).[220]

---

216. Hemmo 2008, 241–242.
217. Norros II 2012, 99.
218. Hemmo 2008, 242.
219. Sisula-Tulokas 2015, 198.
220. Taxell 1972, 139.

246. Although the starting point in Finnish contract law in principle is avoidance of the whole contract, the disputed contracts in (the rather old) Supreme Court decisions KKO 1961 II 100 and KKO 1962 II 80 were – based on section 33 of the Contracts Act (228/1929) – declared invalid only in part.[221]

247. In comparison to Finnish law, partial avoidance seems to have a stronger position in Article II. – 7:213 of DCFR. It states: 'If a ground of avoidance under this Section affects only particular terms of a contract, the effect of an avoidance is limited to those terms unless, giving due consideration to all the circumstances of the case, it is unreasonable to uphold the remaining contract.'

248. The existing grounds for invalidity are sometimes designed to protect public interests, a weaker party, or the interests of a third party and are therefore preferably to be observed ex officio by courts and other authorities. Nonetheless, it is fairly difficult to sufficiently clearly state those situations where this is to happen,[222] and for the most part, the grounds for invalidity are such that they must be invoked. Such grounds are designed to protect private interests and can usually be remedied, for example, through approval or passivity by the injured party: The party who could claim invalidity of a contract based on such a ground may thus choose to treat the contract as valid instead, in case he finds this to be more favourable for him. The classical grounds of invalidity found in sections 28–33 of the Contracts Act are of such kinds, and they have all been discussed above in this chapter. It was also in connection herewith already pointed out that there are grounds for invalidity that cannot be remedied. These are for instance defects in the form in situations where the law requires a particular form to a contract (sale of real estate), contracts with a purpose contrary to the law (someone takes upon himself to commit a crime) or good practice/moral (sexual services are offered against payment), or fictitious (sham) contracts, where the content of the contract does not reflect the real intentions of the parties. Also, contractual arrangements that are contrary to competition law and certain special legislation can be mentioned in connection herewith.

II. Retroactive Effect of Avoidance or Nullity

249. The effects of avoidance in DCFR are regulated in Article II. – 7:212. The said article states: '(1) A contract which may be avoided under this Section is valid until avoided but, once avoided, is retrospectively invalid from the beginning. (2) The question whether either party has a right to the return of whatever has been transferred or supplied under a contract which has been avoided under this Section, or a monetary equivalent, is regulated by the rules on unjustified enrichment. (3) The effect of avoidance under this Section on the ownership of property which has

---

221. *See* DCFR 2009 Volume 1, 528, where this is noted too.
222. According to Ämmälä 1993, 159 a court should examine ex officio at least the basic prerequisites for a contract, that is the legal capacity of the parties to form contracts, other mandatory prerequisites of the contract that are based on the law, as well as whether the content of the contract is in conformity with the law.

been transferred under the avoided contract is governed by the rules on the transfer of property.' Also, Articles II. –7:301 and II. – 7:302 of DCFR on the infringement of fundamental principles and mandatory rules respectively can be mentioned.

250. In Finland, there are no such general rules on the legal consequences of invalidity.[223] However, an invalid contract is unenforceable in court, which means that the parties cannot be obliged to fulfil their commitments based on such a contract. The effect of invalidity is retroactive; the contract is thus, as a main rule, treated as invalid from the beginning. Consequently, in a situation where the avoided contract has already been performed in total or in part, the parties are to make restitution of what they have received under the contract. In addition, it is possible that a party is obliged to pay compensation for the benefit he has had of the already received performance, and he may be entitled to receive compensation for his costs for taking care of the object of the contract. This *ex tunc*-effect of invalidity differs from the *ex nunc*-effect of contract termination, which begins at the time of termination and focuses on the future.[224]

III. Damages

251. When a contract is deemed invalid, damages may be awarded too. According to Finnish contract law, damages are to be paid on the basis of what could be called the reliance interest. The aggrieved party is thus to be compensated in accordance with a hypothetical situation in which no preparations for contract formation has taken place, that is in accordance with the 'negative interest' (in Finnish: *negativinen sopimusetu*). This is, of course, rather logical since an invalid contract is treated as invalid from the very start.[225]

252. This approach differs from the situation, where damages are to be paid in case of contract termination due to breach of contract. In such a situation, the aggrieved party is normally to be compensated with a sum that will put him as nearly as possible into the hypothetical position he would have been in had the contract been duly performed, that is in accordance with the 'positive interest' (in Finnish: *positiivinen sopimusetu*).[226]

---

223. Hemmo I 2003, 319, Sisula-Tulokas 2015, 202.
224. Hemmo I 2003, 321–322, Sisula-Tulokas 2015, 203.
225. *See also* Art. II. – 7:214(2) of DCFR, which states: 'The damages recoverable are such as to place the aggrieved party as nearly as possible in the position in which that party would have been if the contract had not been concluded, with the further limitation that, if the party does not avoid the contract, the damages are not to exceed the loss caused by the mistake, fraud, coercion, threats or unfair exploitation.'
226. Hemmo I 2003, 320, Sisula-Tulokas 2015, 203.

Chapter 3. The Contents of a Contract

§1. The Different Clauses

I. Ascertaining of Express Terms

253. An express term in a contract is usually to be given the meaning that corresponds to its 'normal' meaning in accordance with common language usage. Sometimes, for instance when a term is 'technical' or 'legal' by nature, its meaning in accordance with the common usage within that field will nonetheless prevail (*see* §2 below for more information.)

II. Implied Terms

254. Since contract interpretation in Finland should take into consideration all materials that impact the content of the contract,[227] also possible implied contract terms that are not per se visible in the contract are to be observed. Such terms may exist, for example in flexible, long-term cooperation contracts, where it can be assumed that the contract document will not be exhaustive. For instance, the purpose of the contract – that perhaps is made clear in the preamble to the contract – and the application of the principle of loyalty may give rise to implied terms that the parties must observe.[228]

255. Implicit terms may also exist on the basis of reasonableness: There is, for instance, case law from the Court of Appeal of Kouvola stating that a franchisee in fact has a right to terminate an unprofitable franchise agreement concluded for a period of ten years, even though the contract does not include such a clause. The solution was based on section 36 of the Contracts Act and on the Code of Ethics issued by the Finnish Franchising Association.[229]

III. Standard Terms and Exemption Clauses

256. In Article II. – 1:109 of DCFR, a standard term is defined as 'a term which has been formulated in advance for several transactions involving different parties and which has not been individually negotiated by the parties'. As was already noted above (*see* Chapter 1, §1, I), one cannot find a definition of the said concept in any

---

227. *See* Supreme Court decisions KKO 1990:99 and KKO 2001:34.
228. Sund-Norrgård 2011, 124–125.
229. Decisions 9 Jun. 2005 Nos 640 and 641 of the Court of Appeal of Kouvola. However, a different approach is taken in decisions 10 Jun. 2005 No. 873 (S 03/930) and No. 874 (S 04/140) of the Vaasa Court of Appeal (also concerning the termination right of a franchisee when the franchise contract is concluded for a specific time period).

laws in Finland. This is in itself quite natural due to the fact that the existing contract law provisions, as a starting point, are applicable to both individually negotiated terms and to standard terms. Nevertheless, specific principles for the
interpretation of standard terms do exist. These are needed since there presumably
is a high risk for standard terms being unbalanced. Naturally, the presumption is that
mutually drafted agreed documents are less unbalanced than standard terms provided by only one of the parties.

257. The fundamental problem with standard terms lies in determining whether
or not both parties to the contract have in fact read – and understood – the terms in
question. If a party has not, it is not possible to establish any real common intention/
purpose among the contracting parties as to those terms. The task is thus to decide
whether the standard terms are to be considered binding anyway. Typically, a party
will be bound by such standard terms that are included in a contract document that
he has signed. This is true also for such standard terms that are referred to in the
individually negotiated contract or in an offer, provided that the party in question
has had a real possibility to acquaint himself with the terms before signing the contract. The available time frame, as well as to what degree – if any – the standard
terms may be considered well-known within the field in question, will have an
impact on this contemplation.[230] The situation is less clear if the standard terms are
not included in the contract document but in marketing materials or the like. Standard terms may nonetheless become binding even in a situation where no references to them exist: they may become binding on the basis of commercial practice/
usage or practice established between the parties.[231]

258. The binding effect of standard terms is dependent on issues like the content
of the terms and the identity of the parties: The more unbalanced content, the higher
demands for binding effect. The demands are especially high for terms that can be
described as 'surprising and burdensome' from the point of view of the other party.
Thus, in case that party has no knowledge of such a term, his attention must be especially drawn to it in order for it to become binding upon him. A professional and
otherwise strong party will nevertheless more easily become bound by standard
terms compared to a weaker party (consumer, franchisee or other small entrepreneur).[232]

---

230. Questions like these are discussed in Supreme Court decisions KKO 1993:45 and KKO 2001:126.
231. Wilhelmsson 2008, 66–84, Hemmo 2008, 95–101, Saarnilehto 2009, 63–66, Sund-Norrgård 2014,
    52–55. *See also* DCFR 2009 Volume 1, 591: 'It may follow from a usage that terms which have
    not been individually negotiated may be binding upon a party who did not know of them.'
232. Wilhelmsson 2008, 65–66, Hemmo 2008, 101–105, Saarnilehto 2009, 66, Sund-Norrgård 2014,
    54–55, 119–120.

259. If the standard terms provided by a party are unclear, it is an established principle to interpret them to the detriment of their drafter (*in dubio contra stipulatorem*).[233] Standard terms that favour one of the parties are also to be interpreted narrowly. A narrow interpretation of a clause often means an interpretation in accordance with its wording.[234]

260. Exemption clauses/limitation of liability clauses limit or exclude a party from liability. One may, for example, use maximum liability caps or exclude liability for certain types of damages, such as indirect loss. Exemption clauses can be in the form of standard terms or in the form of individually negotiated terms.[235] Exemption clauses change the normal risk allocation between the contracting parties. As a starting point, they are nonetheless legally binding. According to Supreme Court decision KKO 2012:72, this is true also when the exemption clause/limitation of liability clause is comprehensive, provided that it is sufficiently clear and unambiguous. Certainly, it is possible that section 36 of the Contracts Act is applicable in some situations, and limitation of liability clauses have in fact traditionally been seen as a type of clause that typically will be adjusted in court.[236]

261. As a main rule, a party's liability cannot be limited in case he is guilty of gross negligence.[237] This is a form of negligence that can be placed between 'normal' negligence and intent, nonetheless closer to intent. Based on legal writing, gross negligence may be at hand when a party shows indifference, essentially diverges from the standard of care applicable to a given situation, neglects to undertake measures of precaution needed in order to avoid vast damage, or starts doing a job that requires qualifications that he clearly does not have. A highly qualified person who does not act in accordance with the 'norm' of the field in question is also more easily considered gross negligent than an unqualified non-specialist.[238]

262. Unclear exemption clauses are to be interpreted to the detriment of their drafter (*in dubio contra stipulatorem*), and exemption clauses are also to be interpreted narrowly. According to Supreme Court decision KKO 1992:178, this is especially the case if the clause in question is drafted by only one of the parties and has a general, unclear content.

263. In addition, an exemption clause can be 'surprising and burdensome' from the point of view of the other party. In such a case, his attention must be especially

---

233. The Supreme Court referred to this principle in, for example, decisions KKO 2008:53, KKO 2010:69 and KKO 2016:10. *See also* the discussion in Sund-Norrgård 2014, 114–117 and references.
234. Sund-Norrgård 2014, 117–119 and references.
235. *See* Sund-Norrgård II 2015, 128–140 for examples of different limitation of liability clauses.
236. Government bill 247/1981, 15, Saarnilehto 2009, 176.
237. For information on the discussion (in Sweden) concerning whether this is a correct approach, or whether the problem should be solved solely on the basis of s. 36 of the Contracts Act, *see* Sund-Norrgård II 2015, 124–127 and references.
238. Taxell 1972, 101, Hemmo II 2003, 288, Saarnilehto 2005, 7, Liebkind 2009, 136–137, 140–144, Sund-Norrgård II 2015, 126.

drawn to the clause in order for it to become binding upon him. This is typically so, where the clause essentially diminishes the party's rights or increases his responsibilities in comparison to non-mandatory law or where no such law exists, in comparison to general principles of contract law or an established usage within the field.[239]

IV. Penalty Clauses

264. Penalty clauses/clauses on liquidated damages (in Finnish: *sopimussakkolauseke*) are often used in situations where the (amount of) actual damage is difficult to ascertain. The clause provides for payment of a beforehand agreed upon sum in case of breach of contract. Consequently, there is no need for the injured party to prove the actual damage caused by the breach, and it is quite possible that the party in breach will pay an amount that exceeds the actual damage caused. The party in breach cannot avoid payment by providing proof of the fact that the breach did not cause any damage. As a starting point, it is also irrelevant whether the party in breach has acted negligently or not.[240]

265. It is certainly possible that the penalty clause actually is an exemption clause: This is so if the amount of liquidated damages in a sales contract is low and the clause is intended to exclusively regulate the seller's liability in case of a delay in delivery.[241] If this is what the parties have intended with the clause, there is, as a starting point, no reason to interpret it otherwise. It is nevertheless not always easy to clearly establish the common intention of the parties in a situation like this, and a penalty clause will not always limit the injured party's right to compensation to the agreed amount. It may be of significance in this contemplation if there is a clear discrepancy between the amount of liquidated damages and the real damage that the said breach of contract can be expected to cause. Without such a discrepancy, it is more likely that the amount of liquidated damages in fact will be seen as the maximum amount to be paid in case of breach of contract.[242] It can also be pointed out that a penalty clause in a contract that covers only certain breaches of contract does not hinder the injured party from recovering damages based on other breaches of contract. This is made clear in Supreme Court decision KKO 1986 II 97.[243]

266. Penalty clauses may sometimes be adjusted on the basis of section 36 of the Contracts Act (228/1929, as amended 956/1982), but for instance in decision KKO 2001:27, the Supreme Court decided otherwise. The Supreme Court also

---

239. Sund-Norrgård II 2015, 127 and references.
240. Hemmo II 2003, 335–337, Hemmo 2005, 311, Hemmo 2008, 504–505, Lindfelt 2011, 204, Sund-Norrgård II 2015, 128.
241. Nygren 2002, 221.
242. Hemmo II 2003, 341–343. *See also* DCFR 2009 Volume 1, 964–965: 'In most European systems the stipulated payment replaces the damages for non-performance which the creditor would have recovered. ... In FINNISH and DANISH law the solution depends on the interpretation of the term.'
243. *See also* Hemmo II 2003, 341.

stated here that only rarely is a contract clause (of any kind) to be adjusted. In this case, the sellers of real estate had undertaken to pay liquidated damages to the buyers if the transfer of possession would be delayed for reasons not attributable to the buyers. The sellers' mother, who lived on the premises, refused to move out. For this reason, the transfer of possession was delayed by forty-eight weeks, and the amount of liquidated damages became substantial (close to one-third of the purchase price). The Supreme Court based its decision not to adjust the clause on the fact that clauses of this kind are fairly commonly used in sales of real estate. The Court also stated that the sellers, at the time of the sale, had been able to take into consideration the effects of the mother's possible refusal to move. The sellers could also have limited the actual damage by trying to persuade the mother to move. The conclusion not to adjust the clause was not impacted by the amount of liquidated damages, even though it was probably more substantial than the actual loss that the buyer had suffered due to the delay.

V. Arbitration Clauses

267. Arbitration clauses are very common in commercial contracts.[244] Arbitration can be described as a dispute resolution procedure mainly to be used in resolving commercial disputes and where the authorities play no role. The binding effect of the arbitration award is nonetheless acknowledged by the authorities, and the legal question/point of law that has been resolved through arbitration can normally not be tried again.[245] This latter point is made clear in section 2 of the Arbitration Act (967/1992), according to which '[a]ny dispute in a civil or commercial matter which can be settled by agreement between the parties may be referred for final decision to be made by one or more arbitrators'.

268. Arbitration proceedings can be divided into two main types: 'ad hoc' and 'institutional', where the first one is based on national statutes and the parties' arbitration agreements, and the second – at least in part – uses the services of a separate arbitration institute.[246] In Finland, for instance The Finland Arbitration Institute (FAI), which is part of the Finland Chamber of Commerce, administers arbitrations conducted under its own FAI Arbitration Rules.[247] Another possibility is so-called expedited arbitration under the FAI Expedited Arbitration Rules.[248] This is a procedure mainly designed for a speedy resolution of minor, less complex disputes by a sole arbitrator. The FAI also provides model arbitration clauses on their website.[249]

---

244. *See*, for example, Roschier Disputes Index 2021, https://www.roschier.com/publications/RDI2021/#p=1.
245. Ovaska 2007, 25–26.
246. Ovaska 2007, 125–127.
247. At https://arbitration.fi/arbitration/rules/arbitration-rules/.
248. At http://arbitration.fi/arbitration/rules/rules-for-expedited-arbitration/.
249. At http://arbitration.fi/arbitration/model-arbitration-clauses/.

269. Section 3 of the Arbitration Act is an important one in practice that, for example, has been discussed by the Supreme Court. According to section 3(1), the arbitration agreement is to be concluded in writing, and based on section 3(2) the arbitration agreement is considered as concluded in writing 'if it is contained in a document signed by the parties or in an exchange of letters between the parties'. This is moreover so 'when the parties, by exchanging telegrams or telex messages or documents produced in another such manner, have agreed that a dispute shall be decided by one or more arbitrators'. In addition, according to section 3(3) the requirement of a written arbitration agreement is met 'if an agreement which has been made in the manner mentioned in subsection (2) refers to a document containing an arbitration clause'.

270. In Supreme Court decision KKO 2013:84, these requirements were not actually met, but the arbitration clause was considered binding anyway. The facts of the case were in short the following: There was a contract concluded between limited companies J and M, which gave A the right to purchase the shares of M that J owned. According to the contract, disagreements were to be resolved in arbitration proceedings. The question that the Supreme Court discussed was whether A – who thus was not a party to the contract – was bound by the arbitration clause included in it when he demanded damages of J based on the fact that J had sold the said shares to a third party and thereby was in breach of the contract. The Supreme Court answered this question in the affirmative due to the fact that A's claim for damages was based on an alleged breach of the contract formed between J and M. The assessment of A's claim demanded interpretation of the contract and the right of purchase clause. Consequently, the Supreme Court found that the disagreement in question was based on the contract between J and M, and for this reason was to be resolved in arbitration. A thus had no right to try the dispute in the general court.[250]

271. Despite the many advantages with arbitration – such as the parties' right to appoint the arbitrator(s), and the 'private nature' of arbitration that ensures that third parties will not be present during the proceedings – there are drawbacks as well. A weaker and poorer party may, for instance, prefer court proceedings due to the fact that arbitration in comparison generally is much more expensive.[251] The Supreme Court decisions KKO 1996:27 and KKO 2003:60 are of relevance here. In these decisions, the Supreme Court discussed the reasonableness of arbitration clauses based on section 36 of the Contracts Act.

272. In decision KKO 1996:27, the arbitration clause was included in a franchise agreement between unequal parties, and the Supreme Court specifically stated that it was likely that the franchisee had not been able to actually influence the content of the contract. Despite this, the Supreme Court did not adjust the contract. The basis for this conclusion was that it is not unusual for a commercial contract to

---

250. *See also* Supreme Court decision KKO 2007:18.
251. Halijoki 2000, 206, Sund-Norrgård 2014, 222–224.

include an arbitration clause, and thus such a clause cannot be considered 'surprising and burdensome'. The franchisee in question had also been given the opportunity to acquaint himself with the contract for a period of one week before signing it. The franchisee had had access to legal assistance. Even though the arbitration clause was not adjusted in this case, Hemmo points out that the reasoning of the Supreme Court nonetheless shows a readiness to – at least to some extent – also consider the party and the nature of his activities in the assessment.[252] It can also be noted here that in legal writing, arbitration clauses have been seen as such 'additional' clauses to a contract that are not the object of 'real' pre-contractual negotiations. Arbitration clauses should therefore be easier to adjust than more essential clauses on the rights and obligations of the parties.[253]

273. In decision KKO 2003:60, the Supreme Court decided differently in a case that was also about a possible adjustment of an arbitration clause included in a B2B contract. One of the parties had demanded that the arbitration clause should not be applied since he, after the conclusion of the contract, had become financially distressed. For this reason, the clause had become unreasonable. It was clear that the party in question had no income and no means, and he had been granted a free trial and legal counsel for the proceedings in the Supreme Court, which would not be provided for him in arbitration proceedings. The Supreme Court found it established that he needed legal counsel in order to look after his rights and that he was not able to pay for such service. Consequently, the arbitration clause was found unreasonable and was set aside. Wilhelmsson considers Supreme Court decision KKO 2003:60 somewhat surprising given the fact that the earlier Supreme Court decision KKO 1996:27 showed a rather negative attitude towards adjusting arbitration clauses in B2B contracts,[254] and Saarnilehto describes the more recent decision as one that in this regard significantly improves the situation of a business in financial distress.[255]

274. It can be observed that the threshold for adjusting an arbitration agreement formed *after* a certain dispute has already arisen will be higher compared to adjusting one that is formed for future disputes.[256] In B2C contracts, arbitration clauses for the future are in fact not binding on the weaker consumer. This follows from Chapter 12, section 1d of the Consumer Protection Act (38/1978, as amended 16/1994). It states: 'A term in a contract concluded before a dispute arises, under which a dispute between a business and a consumer shall be settled in arbitration, shall not be binding on the consumer.'

275. Arbitration clauses may moreover be unclear, and it is justified to interpret them to the detriment of the drafter (*in dubio contra stipulatorem*), as well as to interpret them narrowly. A narrow interpretation of a specific clause often means an

---

252. Hemmo I 2003, 33, footnote 41.
253. Saarnilehto 1997, 2–3, Koulu 2008, 48.
254. Wilhelmsson 2005, 411.
255. Saarnilehto 2003, 4.
256. Wilhelmsson 2005, 412.

interpretation in accordance with the wording of it. For arbitration clauses, this ensures that the demands of clarity and predictability that can be placed on such clauses are met: It should be possible for a party to know in advance whether or not a certain dispute will be resolved in arbitration proceedings. It can also be required that a stronger party informs a weaker party of the division of costs in case of arbitration.[257]

§2. INTERPRETATION

276. The goal of contract interpretation is to identify the purpose of the contract, in other words, the common intention of the parties. Finnish contract law does not include a parol evidence rule or similar, according to which the contract interpretation is solely focused on the (four corners of the) contract. To the contrary, for instance the Supreme Court has stated in its decision KKO 2001:34 that not solely the wording of the contract is decisive in the pursuit of the goal of contract interpretation; one must also take into consideration all other materials that impact the content of the contract, such as the negotiations that preceded the contract formation.[258]

277. Having said this, other materials than the written contract document are in practice not always observed in Finland (nor in the other Nordic countries) either. So, despite the fact that the, at least fairly modern, contract law of today certainly renders it possible to take all relevant aspects into consideration when interpreting a contract, the written contract may still be decisive for example in court proceedings.[259] If the interpretation result based on the contract terms is clear, it is in any case difficult to deviate from it with reference to other materials.[260]

278. In principle, the starting point in Finnish contract law is that the purpose of the contract/common intention of the parties shall also prevail in a situation where it does not correspond to the wording of the contract, provided of course that the purpose can be established. The view that the purpose of the contract 'wins' over the contract document is in line with a subjective interpretation method. The said method originates in the principle of freedom of contract and is thereby logical. However, as soon as the parties' opinions as to the content of the contract diverge, the subjective opinions lose a lot of relevance.[261] Consequently, in Finland, contracts are usually interpreted with the so-called objective interpretation method. The goal is then to, on the basis of such documentation and other statements that show the common intention of the parties, establish a kind of 'normal content' of the same

---

257. Koulu 2008, 187–190, Sund-Norrgård 2014, 228–229.
258. *See also* Supreme Court decision KKO 1990:99.
259. Sund-Norrgård 2011, 23 and references.
260. Hemmo 2008, 317–318.
261. Annola 2012, 184.

from the point of view of a 'reasonable third person'. It can certainly be both difficult, as well as irrelevant, to strictly separate the two methods from one another.[262]

279. In any case, the subjective opinions of a party are of little importance if there are numerous parties to a contract if the parties are intended to be exchangeable, and if the intention of the parties does not clearly appear from the contract document, that is when the contract is *not* individually formed. Standard terms drafted by a strong party alone may thus be viewed as the archetype of such terms that need to be interpreted with an objective method.[263] This was made clear also in Supreme Court decision KKO 2000:67, where the court stated that an objective interpretation is justified for such terms that have been formed with a large amount of policyholders in mind. The case was about the interpretation of the terms of a legal protection insurance drafted by an insurance company, and the Supreme Court found it elementary that the terms in question were applied in a uniform manner.[264]

280. The so-called hierarchy of norms is relevant when interpreting a contract. It was already enlightened and will not be discussed here again (*see* Introduction to the Law of Contracts, §10 above). In the interpretation of a B2B contract, the mandatory legislation that must be observed is naturally scarce; there is normally no weak party in need of protection here. Thus, the contract is utterly important, and the natural starting point in the interpretation of a written contract concluded between equal parties is the wording of the contract document. A party claiming that the contract does *not* correspond to the common intention of the parties thus usually has the burden of proof for such a claim.[265] It is, however, considered possible for parties to agree in their contract on the division of the burden of proof.[266]

281. In the – in principle objective – interpretation process focusing on the wording of the contract, an expression/term in the contract is usually to be given the meaning that corresponds to its 'normal' meaning in accordance with common language usage. Sometimes, for instance, when a term is 'technical', 'medical', or 'legal' by nature, its meaning in accordance with the common usage within that field will nonetheless prevail. A term that is used in different contexts in a contract is also normally to be given the same meaning in all those contexts. Such a meaning should 'fit the objectives' of the contract, and it can be specifically noted that a wrong use of a term will not decide the content of the contract (*falsa demonstratio non nocet*).[267]

---

262. Saarnilehto 2009, 153, Annola 2012, 175–176, 181–183. *See also* Sund-Norrgård 2014, 97–100 and references for a discussion on subjective and objective interpretation.
263. Annola 2012, 186–189.
264. *See also* Saarnilehto 2009, 153 about this case.
265. Saarnilehto 2009, 149.
266. Virtanen 2005, 486 and references.
267. Hemmo I 2003, 607–624.

282. Each term of a contract should normally be given importance in the inter-pretation.[268] This thus corresponds to Article II. – 8:106 of DCFR. It states: 'An interpretation which renders the terms of the contract lawful, or effective, is to be preferred to one which would not.'

283. If one of the contract parties is responsible for an unclear term, it is an established principle – especially in case of standard terms – to interpret it to the detriment of its drafter (*in dubio contra stipulatorem*). The Supreme Court referred to this principle in, for example, decisions KKO 2008:53, KKO 2010:69 and KKO 2016:10.[269]

284. It can be specifically noted that the Consumer Protection Act includes the following, in this respect relevant, provision for B2C contracts in Chapter 4, section 3 (38/1978, as amended 1259/1994): 'If a term in a contract referred to in this Act has been drafted in advance without the consumer having been able to influence its contents and if uncertainty arises as to the significance of the term, the term shall be interpreted in favour of the consumer.' This provision was applied by the Supreme Court in, for example, decision KKO 2011:13.

285. As has been discussed, some types of clauses – such as standard terms that favour one party, exemption clauses, and clauses that allow a party to unilaterally modify essential rights and duties – are to be interpreted narrowly. In addition, it can be noted here that the principle of narrow interpretation is generally considered applicable to copyright transfers. This principle that has been confirmed in legisla-tive preparatory works,[270] in case law[271] and in legal writing, means that a copy-right transfer is interpreted narrowly to the advantage of the copyright owner (where he is the weaker party); in case of unclear terms, no other usages than those spe-cifically agreed upon will be considered included in the transfer.[272] A narrow inter-pretation is thus often equivalent to an interpretation in accordance with the wording of the clause.

286. In case of unbalanced contract parties, the general contract law principle 'protection of the weaker party' can be of relevance. The point with the said prin-ciple is to redress the balance in a situation where it has not been possible for the – financially/socially/legally – weaker party to form a just agreement. In other words, a functioning contract is the goal when this principle is applied.

287. The principle of protection of the weaker party has many similarities with the principle of reasonableness found in section 36 of the Contracts Act; it is cer-tainly possible to protect a weaker party also by applying the latter.[273] In decision

---

268. Hemmo I 2003, 618–619.
269. *See also* the discussion in Sund-Norrgård 2014, 114–117 and references.
270. Legislative preparatory works Komiteanmietintö 1953:5, 63 and SOU 1956:25, 277.
271. Supreme Court decisions KKO 1984 II 26 and KKO 2005:92.
272. Sund-Norrgård 2011, 122–127 and references.
273. Pöyhönen 1988, 273–274, Ämmälä I 2000, 98–99, Wuolijoki 2009, 101, Saarnilehto et al. 2012, 101, Sund-Norrgård 2014, 100–101.

KKO 2010:69, the Supreme Court stated that one of the contract parties to the said B2B contract was to be considered weaker, and when the content of the contract was to be established, the principle of protection of the weaker party was used as a guiding principle in the interpretation.[274] When the said principle is applied, it thus implies a deviation from the principle of freedom of contract, and it is unclear to what extent one should protect a weaker party at the expense of freedom of contract.[275]

288. The assumption, especially in B2B contracts, is that the parties have had, and have used, their freedom of contract in the drafting process. Consequently, once a contract has been concluded, it is considered binding upon the parties (*pacta sunt servanda*). In other words, the price of freedom of contract is the binding effect of contract.[276] Nonetheless, the principle of reasonableness found in section 36 of the Contracts Act makes it possible for a court or a court of arbitration to adjust, or set aside, unfair contract terms. This principle has been discussed above (*see*, for instance, Introduction to the Law of Contracts, §1 and §8, and Part I, Chapter 1, §1, IV).

289. In some cases, especially where the parties have formed a long-term, close cooperation based on trust and interdependence, the principle of loyalty influences the contract interpretation. This is logical since a contract of this kind is formed in order to obtain a functioning cooperation between the parties. The focus on risk allocation is often less prominent. This means that not all contracts are drafted with an intention to be as exhaustive as possible, and for instance, Annola stresses the existence of 'dynamic contracts' that are intended to be supplemented during the contract term.[277] The main function of the principle of loyalty is perhaps to act as a support/as a guiding principle in the interpretation of a contract (*see* Introduction to the Law of Contracts, §8 above for more information on the principle of loyalty).

§3. CONDITIONAL CONTRACTS

290. The legal effect of a contract can be made conditional in such a way that it is dependent on a future, uncertain event. Conditions of this kind can be divided into *suspension clauses* and *cancellation clauses*. The parties may, for instance, agree that a sale of real estate will become final provided that the buyer actually gets the loan that he has applied for (suspension clause), or that the sale will be cancelled if the purchase price is not paid on time (cancellation clause).[278]

291. In Finland, the conditional sale of real estate, in the form of suspension and cancellation clauses, is regulated by law. For this reason, these conditional contracts

---

274. Annola 2010, 6–7.
275. Wuolijoki 2009, 102, Saarnilehto et al. 2012, 101.
276. Saarnilehto 2009, 38.
277. Annola 2003, 31, 49–50.
278. Telaranta 1990, 58.

will be further discussed here. Although conditional contracts are often formed in order to secure payment for the seller, it should be stressed that a sale of real estate can be conditional for the benefit of either party to the contract.[279]

292. According to Chapter 2, section 2 of the Code of Real Estate (540/1995), '[a] clause may be taken into the deed of sale to the effect that the sale can be cancelled for a reason not mentioned in this Code or that the seller retain title to the real estate until the price has been paid or another condition fulfilled'. A clause of this kind is nevertheless not binding 'unless it has been taken into the deed of sale, nor in so far as it is intended to remain valid for longer than five years from the conclusion of the sale'. In case the clause lacks a validity period, it is considered valid for five years. It should also be noted that an action for the return of the real estate to the seller must, at the latest, be brought in three months from the end of the validity of the clause. Based on Chapter 4 of the Code of Real Estate, this provision also applies to other conveyances of real estate.

293. Chapter 2, section 14(1) of the Code of Real Estate gives the buyer, after the conclusion of the sale, a right to use the real estate and dispose of it, as well as reconvey his right, despite the fact that retention or transfer of title has been made conditional. However, before the sale is final, he may not, based on section 14(2) (as amended 623/2013) without the consent of the seller, for instance, extract land resources in such a manner that the value of the real estate diminishes significantly, or raise liens over it, or attach special rights to it.

294. The obligation to apply for the registration of title, in accordance with Chapter 11, section 1 of the Code of Real Estate, is applicable also to conditional sales of real estate. This must be done within six months of the drawing up of the deed of conveyance or another document on which the acquisition is based. In case of a conditional sale, the application will, however, be left in abeyance in accordance with Chapter 12, section 2.[280]

295. Another type of clause that could briefly be mentioned in connection herewith is the retention of ownership clause. This is a clause according to which the seller retains ownership of the goods until certain conditions are fulfilled by the buyer, usually payment of the purchase price. It is a fairly common type of clause in a seller's set of standard terms applicable to sales of goods. A problematic issue may thus be the ascertainment of whether or not the said clause is binding upon the buyer. For example, in Supreme Court decision KKO 2001:126, a retention of ownership clause was considered binding, whereas in KKO 1993:45 it was not. The binding effect of standard terms was already discussed in more detail above (*see* Chapter 3, §1, III).

---

279. Kartio 2012, 135.
280. For further discussion about conditional sales of real estate, *see* Kartio 2012.

Chapter 4. Privity of Contract

§1. THE RULE OF PRIVITY OF CONTRACT

I. Third Parties and the Contract

296. According to the privity doctrine, rights and duties originating from a certain contract only affect the parties to that contract. In line with this, a self-evident starting point in Finnish contract law is that only the parties to a contract are bound by it, and they may only contract for themselves.[281] In Finland, the doctrine of privity has nevertheless historically not been interpreted as strictly as in, for example, England,[282] and there are some classical exceptions to the privity doctrine. In this regard, the contract in favour of a third party can be noted, as well as the succession of rights to a third party, giving the transferee the possibility to present contractual claims to the original contracting party. Also, contract conclusion via a representative can be mentioned.[283]

II. Contract for the Benefit of a Third Party

297. An exception from the privity doctrine is thus the contract in favour of a third party. Such contracts have in Finland been accepted for a long time, despite the above-noted starting point that parties can only contract for themselves. Contracting to the *detriment* of a third party is, as a starting point, forbidden.[284] The latter situation is possible on the basis of collective agreements that, despite not being employment contracts, regulate terms and conditions of workplaces. In Finland, collective agreements are regulated in the Collective Agreements Act (436/1946).

298. Actual contracts for the benefit of a third party can be understood as contracts, where a party to the contract, in relation to the other party to the contract, undertakes to perform something to the benefit of an outside third party. Such contracts are in practice often formed in the insurance industry; a third party may be the beneficiary, for instance, in a life insurance contract.[285]

§2. TRANSFER OF CONTRACTUAL RIGHTS

299. Although the group of people that – as creditors or debtors – are affected by obligations normally remain unchanged, changes do happen sometimes. The basis for such changes may be universal succession, which is based on the law only.

---

281. Saarnilehto 2009, 5–7, Kangas 2009, 72, Tammi-Salminen 2010, 373.
282. Kangas 2009, 75.
283. Kangas 2009, 75 and references.
284. Tammi-Salminen 2010, 373, 378, Sund-Norrgård 2016, 591–592. *See also* Art. II. – 9:301 of DCFR on the possibility to 'confer a right or other benefit on a third party'.
285. Norros I 2012, 166–167.

An example is inheritance where the legal status of the diseased passes, with some limitations, to the heirs. Another is merger where all assets and liabilities, contracts with their rights and obligations, will transfer as they are from the merging company to the receiving company.[286] Changes based on universal succession will not be further discussed.

300. The basis for change may be that the right to performance under a contract has been assigned to a third party. As a starting point, a creditor is allowed to freely assign his right to performance, which is also the solution adopted in Article III. – 5:105(1) of DCFR. It states: 'All rights to performance are assignable except where otherwise provided by law.' In Finland, this conclusion can, by analogy, be drawn on the basis of the Promissory Notes Act (622/1947), and in particular on the basis of the part of this act, which deals with so-called non-negotiable promissory notes. It is also made clear in section 27 that assignment normally does not alter the performance. This section states: 'When a non-negotiable promissory note is transferred or assigned, the transferee shall not have a better right against the debtor than the transferor had unless expressly otherwise stipulated.'[287]

301. Some rights are personal to the creditor and therefore not freely assignable. One example of this is the main rule concerning assignment of rights and obligations for both parties under a contract of employment in Chapter 1, section 7(1) of the Employment Contracts Act (55/2001). It states: 'The parties to the contract of employment shall not assign any of their rights or obligations under a contract of employment to a third party without the other party's consent, unless otherwise provided below.'

302. Article III. – 5:109(1) of DCFR can be noted in this regard. It states: 'A right is not assignable if it is a right to a performance which the debtor, by reason of the nature of the performance or the relationship between the debtor and the creditor, could not reasonably be required to render to anyone except that creditor.' A change of debtor requires two, or sometimes even three, separate legal acts. First, the new debtor must, in relation to the creditor, commit to what the previous debtor had committed to. This commitment does not in itself require the creditor's consent. The creditor may nonetheless, as is the case also in Article III. – 5:203(3) of DCFR, reject the right conferred against the new debtor.[288] Second, the creditor must, usually expressly, discharge the previous debtor from the obligation to perform. If this does not happen, and the new debtor has committed to the same performance, the debtors are jointly responsible for the performance.[289] Third, in some situations, the previous debtor must approve the discharge and give up his right to perform.[290]

---

286. Norros I 2012, 147–148.
287. There are exceptions also to this main rule, *see* Norros I 2012, 150–158.
288. Norros II 2012, 244.
289. Norros II 2012, 244–245.
290. Norros II 2012, 246–247.

303. In addition to the assignment of mere rights and/or obligations under a contract, it is also possible to transfer the whole contractual position of a party, that is, both the rights and the obligations, to a third party. In principle, the same pattern as discussed applies also to such a situation, albeit there may be provisions in specific acts that alter the outcome. For instance, based on section 44 of the Act on Residential Leases (481/1995), a lessee is not allowed to transfer his leasehold to a third party without permission from the lessor. Section 45 nevertheless allows him to 'transfer a leasehold to his or her spouse or a child of their family or the parent of either spouse if the transferee is living in the apartment, unless the lessor has justifiable cause for contesting such transfer'. Another example is the transfer of licensing agreements. Namely, despite the fact that patents, trademarks, copyrights and other IPRs are usually freely transferable, licensing agreements are normally not.[291]

§3. THE SPECIAL CASE OF A 'SUB-CONTRACT', E.G., THE (NOMINATED) SUBCONTRACTOR IN BUILDING CONTRACTS

304. Normally, a party to a contract may use a third party for the performance of his obligations under the contract. Due to the fact that the debtor, as a strong main rule, is responsible for the performance of an assistant/subcontractor in the same way that he is responsible for his own performance, the position of the creditor is not weakened by such an arrangement. This arrangement is nevertheless forbidden, where the main contract requires a personal performance of the debtor or where subcontracting is prohibited by statutory law or by express contract terms.[292]

305. The employee's right to use an assistant may serve as an example of a situation of this kind, which is regulated by law. Chapter 1, section 8 of the Employment Contracts Act (55/2001) states: 'If, with the employer's consent, the employee has hired an assistant to help him/her to fulfil his or her obligations under the contract of employment, the person hired as assistant also has an employment relationship with the employer which has thus given consent.'

306. The General Conditions for Building Contracts formed in 1998 (in Finnish: *Rakennusalan yleiset sopimusehdot*, YSE 1998), which at the moment can be considered the most important existing set of standard terms within the field in question, will shortly be addressed as well. It is made clear in YSE 1998 that a contractor is liable for the works and actions of his subcontractors: In accordance with sections 7.3 and 7.4 of YSE 1998, the contractor is obliged 'to put forward his most important sub-contractors and sub-suppliers for the approval of the client in sufficient time before engaging them'. However, despite the fact that approval of subcontractors and sub-suppliers 'can be refused only where there is good cause', such approval 'does not diminish the liability of the contractor'.

---

291. *See* the discussion in Sund-Norrgård 2011, 238–241 and references.
292. Norros I 2012, 132–133.

307. In the glossary of YSE 1998, the contractor is defined as 'the client's contracting party who undertakes to achieve the finished result defined in the contract documents'. There are three sub-categories of contractors: The first is the main contractor (in Finnish: *pääurakoitsija*), which is defined as 'the contractor in a contractual relationship with the building owner and who is named in commercial documents as the main contractor, and who is charged with the site management duties to the extent defined in the contract'. The second is the nominated subcontractor (in Finnish: *sivu-urakoitsija*), which is defined as a 'contractor undertaking work that does not form part of the main building contract and who is in a contractual relationship with the building owner'. Finally, the subcontractor (in Finnish: *aliurakoitsija*) is defined as 'a second contractor undertaking work commissioned by the contractor'. There is thus no contractual relationship between the contractor and the nominated subcontractor. Nevertheless, based on section 4 of YSE 1998 site management duties, such as 'drawing up of site construction schedule' and 'arrangement and co-ordination of work on the site' are the responsibilities of the main contractor, and the nominated subcontractors and subcontractors are obliged to follow the directions on such issues given by the contractor. The possible consequences of, for instance, this arrangement on site – with or without subordination of nominated subcontracts – will not be discussed further.

§4. *ACTIO PAULIANA* DOES NOT EXIST IN FINNISH CONTRACT LAW

308. The remedy *actio pauliana*, originating in Roman law, does not exist in Finnish contract law. In those systems where it does exist, it may give the creditor an action against the contract party holding the property, where the purpose of the contract is to disadvantage/defraud the creditor by putting the said property beyond his reach. It can be noted that *actio pauliana* is very closely linked to insolvency law and is therefore not either explicitly dealt within DCFR.[293]

---

293. DCFR 2009 Volume 1, 39.

Chapter 5. The Termination of the Contract

§1. PERFORMANCE AND BREACH

309. There is a breach of contract when the contract in question is not performed correctly. This may be the result where a party has failed to act or has acted in some other way than the fulfilment of the contract in question presupposes.[294]

310. In accordance with the so-called correspondence theory (in Finnish: *vastaavuusteoria*), a performance is faulty where it, to the detriment of its receiver, diverges from what the party obligated to perform ought to do.[295] The theory has been criticized in legal writing for not offering an answer to the question of what the party obligated to perform actually is supposed to do: Many times, the most difficult task in case of breach of contract is to define the performance, since this may require contract interpretation as well as gap filling.[296] In this day and age, it can also be relevant to ask whether the climate impact of goods sold may in fact constitute a defect.[297]

311. A breach of contract may be the result where a primary obligation of the contract, as well as where an ancillary obligation is neglected.[298] There nonetheless exists a tolerance limit which, at least to some extent, hinders opportunistic, speculative demands based on faulty performance. The contract is thus considered fulfilled even though the performance slightly differs from the agreed.[299]

§2. IMPOSSIBILITY, FRUSTRATION AND HARDSHIP: 'THE UNFORESEEN'

312. Finnish contract law does not embrace the German doctrine *Wegfall der Geschäftsgrundlage* or the common law doctrine of frustration as such.[300] There is no clear definition of hardship to be found in Finnish law either. 'The unforeseen' may nevertheless have an impact on the obligations of a party to a contract, and clauses on both force majeure and hardship are certainly included in many contracts.

313. A hardship clause usually imposes a duty to renegotiate the contract terms in the case of exceptionally changed circumstances. The force majeure clause is,

---

294. Taxell 1972, 7–9, Taxell 1997, 77.
295. Routamo 1980, Hemmo II 2003, 112.
296. Hemmo II 2003, 113–114, Sund-Norrgård 2011, 206 and references.
297. Sisula-Tulokas 2020.
298. Taxell 1972, 175.
299. Hemmo II 2003, 114–117.
300. Under the latter, according to Davies on Contract 2004, 256, 'the parties to a contract are excused further performance of their obligations if some event occurs during the currency of the contract, without the fault of either party, which makes further performance impossible or illegal, or which makes it something radically different from what was originally undertaken'.

however, the most commonly used clause type dealing with changed circumstances. The idea is that an event that qualifies as force majeure will exempt a party from the obligation to perform on time or will exempt him from liability to pay damages in case of delay. There are differing opinions presented in legal writing on how to properly define force majeure, and it may also be difficult to draw a line between force majeure and hardship. At the moment, there is an ongoing discussion on how to interpret force majeure in the context of the COVID-19 pandemic. For instance, it may be problematic that force majeure-clauses often are boilerplate-clauses that have not been the focus of the parties' attention during negotiations: It may thus be problematic to find out the parties' actual intent regarding force majeure, for example, when faced with a pandemic. Moreover, one can probably not draw the conclusion that there is force majeure in a situation where the lessee in a commercial lease has lost customers as a result of the pandemic. But does this mean that the contractual balance between the lessor and the lessee is disrupted in such a way that the rent is to be modified (on other grounds)?[301] It is nevertheless clear that objective impossibility is not needed in order for an event to qualify as force majeure. It can be noted that when used extensively (events that do not really qualify as force majeure are treated as such), the force majeure clause is in fact a limitation of liability clause.[302]

314. The starting point in Finnish contract law is that a party is to perform the contract even if performance has become more onerous than he expected when the contract was formed. Due to the fact that a contract – especially one that is drafted comprehensively – may be the result of conscious risk allocation and risk taking, it is for example important that courts do not too often adjust the contract terms based on section 36 of the Contracts Act (228/1929, as amended 956/1982). Such adjustment is nevertheless possible: According to the wording of the said section, in determining what is unfair, regard shall also be had to circumstances prevailing after the conclusion of the contract.

315. Although the need to adjust contract terms based on changed circumstances is more likely to be present in the case of long-term contracts compared to short-term contracts,[303] it should be stressed that long-term contracts often are formed with the notion that things may change during the contract term. For this reason, it is possible to assume that for such contracts *clausula rebus sic stantibus*, that is, that contracts are to be performed if circumstances stay essentially the same, has in fact been replaced by the understanding that circumstances are likely to change all the time.[304] Thus, for contracts of this kind, it may be even more difficult to differentiate between 'normal' business risks that do not influence the party's obligation to perform and such exceptional changes for which the party is not accountable.[305] The reason for the change is of importance in the contemplation. A

---

301. Hoppu 2020.
302. Sund-Norrgård II 2015, 136–137 and references.
303. Wilhelmsson 2008, 132.
304. Jokela 1978, 136, Grönfors 1995, 21–23, Keskitalo 2000, 16–17.
305. Edlund 2009, 436.

seller, for example, is often considered to bear the risk of not getting a vital permit from a public authority. Also, price fluctuations and exchange rate changes are often considered as normal risks. Amendments of the law are often treated as unforesee-able changes.[306]

316. In order for changed circumstances to be of judicial importance, they must significantly impact the contract. As a starting point, it is also required that a party has not foreseen, and should not have foreseen, the development that has occurred. Moreover, the event is to have been caused by something beyond the party's control. In other words, the party has not been able to prevent the event or its harmful effects.

317. If a party has indeed foreseen – or should have foreseen – the development in question, one may, for instance, argue that he should have made an adequate reservation in the contract in order not to be held accountable. In such cases, the change may be considered to be within the bounds of possibility for a contract of that kind. Consequently, a party may be held accountable due to the fact that one can assume that he has been aware of the problem but consciously took the risk that the contract may not become as lucrative as he possibly hoped. Naturally, one must keep in mind the difficulty of separating events within a party's control from those beyond a party's control.[307]

318. Supreme Court decision KKO 1990:124 can be observed in connection with a discussion on the impact of changed circumstances. A Finnish association with roots in Vyborg (Russia) had, on the basis of a contract formed with the city of Hämeenlinna, left their art in the care of the city's art museum, where it would be stored and exhibited. The term of validity of the contract was not specified, and the contract did not include any stipulation as to the association's right to demand the art back. The ownership of the art remained with the association. The purpose of the contract was to further the interests of both parties. The association was given the storage space it needed for the art, and the art also turned out to be important for the city: it came to have an essential impact on the realization of a new museum in which the said art was later placed. Since the city had arranged for suitable exhibition grounds to showcase the art, had insured it, etc. the association was not, solely based on ownership, entitled to demand the art back whenever it wanted to. At the same time, it was not possible to draw the conclusion that the parties had intended for the contractual relationship to continue unchanged despite changed circumstances. Thus, when the association after thirty years demanded that the city would give back some of the works of art, the city was instructed by the Supreme Court to do so based on the fact that the city had had possession of the art for a long time and had benefited from the exhibitions. The art was not either anymore as vital for the existence of the city's museum as it had been when the contract was concluded. The association wanted the art back in order to place it in an art museum in southern Karelia due to geographical ties with the association's original domicile. It

---

306. Sund-Norrgård 2011, 230 and references.
307. Keskitalo 2000, 20, Sund-Norrgård 2011, 231 and references.

was concluded that the demand was in line with the association's field of activities, which was to further the interest for art, practice of art and collecting domestic works of art, especially works of art by Karelian artists.

319. Section 27 of the Sale of Goods Act (355/1987) is an example of how issues of 'force majeure type' are dealt with in Finnish law. It states: 'The buyer is entitled to damages for losses that he suffers because of the seller's delay in delivery, unless the seller proves that the delay was due to an impediment beyond his control which he could not reasonably be expected to have taken into account at the time of the conclusion of the contract and whose consequences he could not reasonably have avoided or overcome.' It can be noted here also that according to section 22 of the Sale of Goods Act, the situation in which the goods are not delivered at all is on an equal footing with the situation where the delivery is (merely) delayed. When contemplating the seller's delay as such, the reason for it is not relevant: the concept of delay is objective, and a breach of contract is at hand even though the delivery is delayed for example due to an impediment beyond the seller's control. Such an impediment nonetheless impacts the buyer's right to demand damages (section 27).[308] The buyer is moreover not entitled to hold to the contract and to require its performance in case of an impediment that the seller cannot overcome (section 23). Objective impossibility is not required here; the seller may thus refer to such essential obstacles for delivery that concern only him (his factory is destroyed in a fire, etc.).[309]

320. The risk allocation between seller and buyer is tied to the time when the risk passes from the seller to the buyer. The risk usually passes when the goods are delivered (section 13 of the Sale of Goods Act), and the fact that this is the crucial point in time for the risk allocation is made clear in section 21. It states: 'Whether the goods are defective shall be determined with regard to their properties at the time when the risk passes to the buyer. The seller is liable for any defect that existed at that time even if it did not appear until later.'[310] In other words, as follows from section 12, '[i]f the goods are at the risk of the buyer, he must pay the price even if the goods deteriorate or are destroyed, lost or diminished, provided that the loss or damage is not due to an act or omission of the seller'.

321. Even the liability to pay liquidated damages can be impacted in case of force majeure: it is not considered to be in line with how one normally perceives risk allocation to conclude that the debtor is responsible for force majeure.[311]

322. Finally, the traditional Scandinavian – perhaps mostly Danish and Swedish – so-called doctrine of failed assumptions (in Finnish: *edellytysoppi*, in Swedish

---

308. Also in the case of defects, the buyer's right to demand damages is impacted by the existence of an impediment beyond the seller's control (s. 40, which refers to s. 27).
309. Wilhelmsson et al. 2006, 54–55, 64–66.
310. The risk for the goods is discussed in, for example, Wilhelmsson et al. 2006, 47–52.
311. Taxell 1972, 444, Hemmo II 2003, 340.

förutsättningsläran[312] can be observed. This doctrine has been seen as a complement to the grounds for invalidity in sections 28–33 of the Contracts Act (228/1929). It increases the possibilities for parties to get out of contracts on the basis of mistakes or changed circumstances.[313] The approach to the doctrine has in Finland been rather restrictive (*see also* Chapter 2, §2, I above).[314]

§3. DISCHARGE BY AGREEMENT

323. Since a contract is formed by an agreement between two or more parties it can normally also be brought to an end/discharged by a mutual agreement. The question of discharges in connection with the transfer of contractual rights was already discussed (*see* Chapter 4, §2 above).

324. It is even possible to end an employment contract by mutual agreement, despite that the employer, according to Chapter 7, section 1 of the Employment Contracts Act (55/2001) 'shall not terminate an indefinitely valid employment contract without proper and weighty reason'. When the parties agree to end the employment contract they are not, as a starting point, bound by the termination grounds, periods of notice, nor the course of action found in the said act. Normally a compensation clause is included in the agreement, unclear receivables are explained, and the parties mutually agree to give up obligations that arise from the employment contract.[315]

---

312. *See also* DCFR 2009 Volume 1, 464, 486.
313. Ramberg & Ramberg 2016, 211–214.
314. Hemmo 2008, 231, Sund-Norrgård 2011, 231 and references.
315. For further information on issues of this kind, *see* Tiitinen & Kröger 2012, 482–484 and references. *See* also the very informative Supreme Court decision KKO 2019:76.

Chapter 6. Remedies

§1. General Provisions

325. As a general rule, breach of contract by one party gives the other party recourse to remedies. The available remedies nonetheless differ depending on the type of contract, type of breach and the other party's demands.[316] In order to simplify the discussion and thereby make it easier to grasp, it is mostly focused on sales of goods.

326. Wilhelmsson et al. present the following conclusions based on the provisions of the Sale of Goods Act (355/1987): In case of seller's delay in delivery, the buyer has two main options: (1) he may hold to the contract and require its performance, and in addition demand damages and withhold payment, or (2) he may avoid the contract, and in addition demand damages and withhold payment.[317]

327. In case of defects in the goods, the buyer may (1) require the seller to remedy the defect or to deliver substitute goods, or (2) require a reduction in the contract price, or (3) declare the contract avoided. In addition, he may claim damages and also withhold payment. Remedying the defect or delivering substitute goods are considered to be primary remedies in relation to price reduction and contract avoidance, whereas price reduction and contract avoidance are alternative remedies. Damages may be demanded in addition to the other remedies, and the buyer may also withhold payment.[318]

328. Where the buyer fails to pay the price when it is due, the seller usually has the following two options: (1) he may require payment and claim interest (and occasionally also damages), or (2) he may be entitled to declare the contract avoided as well as to claim damages. In addition, he may withhold control over the goods.[319]

§2. Specific Performance and Its Enforcement

329. The right to hold to the contract and demand specific performance is a general starting point in Finnish contract law: It is thus possible to demand that a specific object is to be delivered, that a specific service is to be performed, or that a passive duty – based on a non-compete clause for instance – is to be fulfilled as agreed.[320] Section 23(1) of the Sale of Goods Act (355/1987) can be observed. The buyer is, if the goods are not delivered or if their delivery is delayed, 'entitled to hold to the contract and to require its performance'. Section 52(1) correspondingly

---

316. Saarnilehto 2009, 188.
317. Wilhelmsson et al. 2006, 57.
318. Wilhelmsson et al. 2006, 117.
319. Wilhelmsson et al. 2006, 162.
320. Hemmo II 2003, 195.

gives the seller 'the right to hold to the contract and to demand payment of the price' in case of the buyer's breach of contract.

330. There are limitations on the right to specific performance in Finnish contract law. One may distinguish between limitations that originate in the type of obligation at hand and those that stem from an impediment to performance. The first type, which is considered to violate the personal freedom of the debtor, include such obligations that require work or service to be performed by a certain natural person or obligations that require his creative contribution. It is not always possible to demand specific performance of ancillary duties either. Limitations of the second kind stem from the impossibility to perform as agreed (the object in question is destroyed in a fire) or from the excessive difficulty of performance.[321] Such limitations are laid down in section 23(1) of the Sale of Goods Act as follows: 'The seller is, nevertheless, not obliged to perform the contract if there is an impediment that he cannot overcome or if the performance would require sacrifices that are disproportionate to the buyer's interest in performance by the seller.'

331. The right to specific performance can be enforced. According to Chapter 2, section 3 of the Enforcement Code (705/2007), '[a] legally final judgment shall be enforced without the applicant being required to post security'. Chapter 2, section 7 is of relevance too. It states: 'A non-final judgment of a District Court where the respondent is ordered to relinquish to the applicant certain chattels may be enforced if the applicant posts security for the return of the assets and for costs. In other cases the bailiff shall at the request of the applicant ensure the preservation of the assets until the judgment becomes final, observing in so far as appropriate the provisions in Chapter 8 on the precautionary seizure of chattels.'

332. There is also a judicial penalty in the form of a threat of a fine (in Finnish: *uhkasakko*). Based on Chapter 3, section 74 of the Enforcement Code '[a] threat of a fine imposed by the bailiff in accordance with this Act shall be imposed either as a fixed amount or as determined by the lapse of time (threat of an accruing fine)'.

333. Section 50 of the Sale of Goods Act, according to which the buyer must collect or take over the goods, can also be noted: This is *not* considered to be such an obligation, the specific performance of which can be enforced by a court order.[322]

§3. TERMINATION

334. The discussion below focuses on the situation where a party to the contract terminates it with immediate effect – that is without a period of notice – due to the other party's breach of contract (in Finnish: *purku/purkaminen*).

---

321. Hemmo II 2003, 195–199.
322. Wilhelmsson et al. 2006, 176.

335. It is a general contract law principle that contracts may be terminated with immediate effect only in case of a fundamental breach of contract.[323] In section 25(1) of Sale of Goods Act (355/1987), this principle is included. The section states: 'The buyer may declare the contract avoided on account of the seller's delay in delivery if the breach of contract is of substantial importance to the buyer and the seller knew or ought to have known this.' Since it is demanded here that 'the seller knew or ought to have known' that the delay constitutes a substantial breach from the point of view of the buyer, it can be crucial for the buyer to – for instance in the contract – draw the seller's attention to the importance of a timely delivery: even a short delay may be substantial in a situation, where the buyer needs the goods on a specific date.[324]

336. Since the requirement based on section 25(1) is rather general by nature, it has been specified by giving the buyer the possibility to declare the contract avoided where the goods are not delivered despite that 'the buyer has fixed an additional period of time for the delivery and the time is not unreasonably short' (section 25(2)). The additional period for delivery must thus be specified in time, and it cannot be unreasonably short. What is considered a long enough additional period of time depends on the case at hand.[325]

337. In the case of defects in the goods, section 39(1) of the Sale of gods Act is applicable. In a similar fashion as the already observed section 25(1), it states: 'The buyer may declare the contract avoided on account of a defect in the goods if the breach of contract is of substantial importance to him and the seller knew or ought to have known this.'

338. Section 54 gives the seller a right of avoidance because of the buyer's substantial delay in payment, whereas avoidance due to the buyer's lack of cooperation is regulated in section 55 (the buyer fails to cooperate as demanded in section 50, or is delayed in collecting or taking over the goods).

339. It should be specifically noted that in those cases, where the goods have already been handed over to the buyer, 'the seller may declare the contract avoided only if he has reserved himself such right in the contract or if the buyer rejects the goods' (section 54(4) of the Sale of Goods Act).

340. The provisions on anticipatory breach in Chapter 11 of the Sale of Goods Act could also be mentioned: section 62 gives the right to avoidance even prior to the date of performance in case 'it becomes clear that a breach of contract entitling a party to avoidance will take place'. Such avoidance is nonetheless without effect 'if the other party immediately provides adequate assurance of his performance'.

---

323. Taxell 1972, 205, 211, Hemmo II 2003, 350.
324. Wilhelmsson et al. 2006, 70.
325. Wilhelmsson et al. 2006, 71.

341. Despite the general principle that termination with immediate effect requires fundamental breach, the equal parties to a B2B contract may relatively freely include termination grounds in their contract, that is also such grounds that otherwise would not qualify as fundamental breaches. However, in the case of long-term contracts, as well as in those cases where many parties cooperate, the right to terminate the contract has in legal writing been seen as rather limited. This is due to the fact that the consequences of termination may otherwise become (too) severe.[326]

342. If a party acts fraudulently or with a purpose to harm the other contract party, there may be a right to terminate with immediate effect also if the breach in itself is not fundamental. The termination right is thus expanded in such cases.[327]

343. The assessment of whether or not a breach of contract is fundamental is nevertheless made from the point of view of the suffering party: Termination is thus allowed if it, all things considered, must be deemed unfair to require him to continue the contractual relationship despite the breach.[328]

344. Following termination, the situation should – where possible – be restored as it was before the contract was concluded.[329] A few illuminating provisions in this regard are found in the Sale of Goods Act: According to section 64(1), '[a]voidance of the contract releases the seller from his obligation to hand over the goods and the buyer from his obligation to pay the price and to take delivery'. Moreover, section 64(2) states: 'Insofar as the contract has been performed, each party is entitled to claim restitution from the other party of whatever the latter party has received. ... ' Based on section 65(1), the buyer must, if the contract is declared avoided, 'account to the seller for any yield he has derived from the goods as well as pay reasonable compensation for any other benefit he may have derived from the goods'.[330] In case the seller is to refund the price, he must, based on section 65(2), 'pay interest on the amount to be refunded in accordance with section 3(2) of the Interest Act (633/1982) from the date on which he received the payment'.

345. In many long-term contracts, it is impossible to restore the situation as it was before the contract's conclusion. Consequently, such contracts are considered to have had full legal effect up until termination.[331]

346. In Finland, as well as in the other Nordic countries, termination is also normally understood as 'partial' in the sense that a contractual penalty clause/liquidated damages clause and other kinds of claims for compensation (damages) can be invoked despite termination.[332] Many long-term contracts, such as licensing

---

326. *See* the discussion in Sund-Norrgård 2011, 209–213 and references.
327. Taxell 1972, 222.
328. Sund-Norrgård 2011, 209–210 and references.
329. Taxell 1972, 201 and Supreme Court decision 1984 II 198.
330. For additional information on this, *see* Wilhelmsson et al. 2006, 134–135.
331. Taxell 1972, 203–204.
332. Taxell 1972, 172, 177, 201–202, Hemmo II 2003, 349.

agreements, also often contain other kinds of explicit clauses on the rights and obligations of the parties post-termination.[333]

§4. *Exceptio Non Adimpleti Contractus* (The Defence of Non-Performance by the Other Party)

347. If the parties have not agreed otherwise, the presumption in the Sale of Goods Act (355/1987) is that the parties should perform the contract simultaneously (the so-called *Zug-um-zug* –principle).[334] Sections 10 and 49 of the said act are relevant in this regard. Based on section 10, the seller 'is not required to hand over the goods nor, by handing over documents or otherwise, to release his control over the goods until the price is paid'. Correspondingly, based on section 49(1), 'the buyer is not obliged to pay before the goods are made available for him or have been placed at his disposal in accordance with the contract'. This, of course, means that in case of the seller's delay in delivery, the buyer's payment of the price will be delayed too.

348. The buyer's right to withhold payment is specifically regulated in section 42(1), which states: 'If the buyer has a claim against the seller on account of a delay in delivery or a defect in the goods, the buyer may withhold payment of the price in an amount corresponding to his claim.' Thus, when the buyer subsequently (i.e., when the goods are delivered, or at a later stage) pays the price, he can make a deduction for his claims based on, for instance, a liquidated damages clause, which often is included in the contract in order to protect the buyer against the seller's delay. Self-evidently the late payment of the purchase price will not in such cases give the seller a right to remedies. However, the buyer bears the risk for both the grounds and the amount: If it later turns out that the buyer incorrectly withheld a part of the payment, the seller may claim penal interest for this overdue payment.[335]

349. The provisions on anticipatory breach in Chapter 11 of the Sale of Goods can be noted also, since they include the right of stoppage: Based on section 61(1), there may be a right to suspend one's own performance in case there are strong reasons to anticipate that the other party will in fact fail to perform a substantial part of his obligations.

§5. Faulty Behaviour of the Debtor

350. Sometimes, a contract party does not have recourse to remedies due to the fact that he himself is guilty of faulty behaviour. One such example was already mentioned (*see* §4 above): a seller, who is in delay with delivery, cannot claim interest for overdue payment from a buyer that has withheld payment based on the delay.

---

333. Sund-Norrgård 2011, 207–208.
334. Wilhelmsson et al. 2006, 44.
335. Wilhelmsson et al. 2006, 96–97.

Another example is found in section 20(1) of the Sale of Goods Act (355/1987), according to which 'the buyer may not rely on a defect which he cannot have been unaware of at the time of the conclusion of the contract'. It is normal for a buyer to examine the goods before purchase, and if he does, he is expected to be thorough. If he fails to meet the standard, he may not, based on section 20(2), 'rely on a defect that he ought to have discovered in the examination'. In other words, such an examination – or lack thereof – may impact the assessment of defects.[336] However, this conclusion is valid 'unless the seller's conduct was incompatible with honour and good faith'. The seller's reprehensible conduct is thus of relevance in this contemplation.

351. The buyer's obligation to examine the goods *after* delivery (sections 31 and 32 of the Sale of Goods Act) is discussed below (*see* §6). Already here, it is nevertheless of importance to observe section 33 of the Sale of Goods Act. This provision makes it clear that a buyer, who has not given notice as required in section 32, is still 'entitled to rely on a defect if the seller is guilty of gross negligence or conduct which is incompatible with honour and good faith'.

352. Also, section 35 of the Sale of Goods Act can be mentioned: the obligation for a buyer to, within a reasonable time, give notice of his actual claims due to a defect 'does not apply if the seller has made himself guilty of gross negligence or conduct which is incompatible with honour and good faith'.

353. In connection with a discussion on faulty behaviour of the debtor, section 70(1) of the Sale of Goods Act on the mitigation of loss is to be noted as well. It states: 'The injured party must take reasonable measures to mitigate his loss.' An injured party that fails to do so is to bear the corresponding part of the loss himself.

§6. Limitations of Actions

354. A contract may become void due to the parties' mutual passivity (in Finnish: *raukeaminen*),[337] and a party's passivity may certainly impact his right to performance on the basis of the contract, as well as his right to remedies due to breach of contract.

355. According to section 23(3) of the Sale of Goods Act (355/1987), '[t]he buyer loses his right to require performance of the contract if he defers his claim for an unreasonably long time'. Moreover, if the seller for example asks the buyer whether he, despite the delay, will accept performance within a certain period of time, and the buyer fails to respond within a reasonable time after he received the

---

336. Wilhelmsson et al. 2006, 110. It should be noted that there is not a general duty for the buyer to examine the goods before purchase. Such a duty will emerge if the seller exhorts him to examine the goods, or such a sample of the goods, where the defects would have appeared (s. 20(3) of the Sale of Goods Act).

337. Hemmo 2008, 530–531, 545.

request, the buyer may not, according to section 24 of the Sale of Goods Act, declare the contract avoided if the seller performs the contract within that period of time.

356. Based on section 31 of the Sale of Goods Act, the buyer is obliged to, after the goods have been delivered, 'as soon as is practicable in the circumstances, examine them in accordance with proper usage'. Due to an authenticity guarantee given by the seller, the buyer of a painting was nevertheless, in Supreme Court decision KKO 1998:150, freed from the obligation to examine the goods as required in section 31(1) of the Sale of Goods Act. The aforementioned obligation to examine the goods is an important one since the buyer, according to section 32 of the Sale of Goods Act 'loses the right to rely on a defect if he does not give notice to the seller of the defect within a reasonable time after he discovered or ought to have discovered it'. It is unclear what is meant by this reasonable time requirement, but in B2B sales contracts, it is not very long, perhaps one to two weeks.[338] In the Finnish Sale of Goods Act, there is thus no equivalence to the maximum two-year period for giving the seller notice found in Article 39(2) of the CISG.

357. Based on section 35 of the Sale of Goods Act, the buyer 'loses his right to require that the defect be remedied, or that substitute goods be delivered if he fails to give notice of such claim to the seller in conjunction with his notice of defect or within a reasonable time thereafter'.

358. Supreme Court decision KKO 2009:61 is an interesting one about the obligation to give notice found in the Consumer Protection Act (38/1978). Chapter 5, section 16(1) of the said act (as amended 16/1994 and 1258/2001) states: 'The buyer shall not invoke a defect in the goods if he/she does not notify the seller of the same within a reasonable time after he/she discovered or ought to have discovered the defect. However, the notice of defect may always be given within two months of the buyer's discovery of the defect; it may also be given to the business who has sold the goods on behalf of the seller or assumed liability for the characteristics of the goods.' The Supreme Court found in this case that the buyer of a horse had in fact given notice as required in the said provision when a veterinary, four months after the sale, in the presence of both the seller and the buyer, had ascertained that the horse suffered from degenerative arthritis.

359. A seller naturally needs to be active too. For instance, according to section 52(3) of the Sale of Goods Act he, where the goods have not yet been delivered, 'loses his right to demand payment of the price if he defers his claim for an unreasonably long time'. The actual length of this unreasonably long time is to be decided case by case.[339]

---

338. Wilhelmsson et al. 2006, 121–122, Norros II 2012, 320.
339. Wilhelmsson et al. 2006, 163.

360. Ultimately, the provisions of the general[340] Finnish Act on the Statute of Limitations (728/2003) limit, for example, a buyer's possibilities to take action: the general period of limitation of three years (section 4) will, concerning compensation for breach of contract, begin when the buyer has noticed the defect in the purchased goods (section 7).[341] The act is applicable to the limitation of debt, by which is meant monetary debts as well as other obligations (section 1(1)). This broad definition encompasses both positive and negative obligations and obligations that are contract based as well as those that are not: for instance an obligation to pay for damages and injuries that are non-contractual is covered too.[342] Based on section 1(2), the act does not, however, apply to taxes, public charges, fines, pensions and the like. The said act is mandatory legislation in the sense that one may not deviate from its provisions to the detriment of the debtor (section 3(1)), and thus it is, for example, not possible to extend the period of limitation or lower the demands for interrupting the period of limitation by contract. As a starting point, it is nevertheless possible to deviate from the provisions to the detriment of the creditor.[343]

§7. DAMAGES AND EXEMPTION CLAUSES

361. As was already discussed (*see* Introduction to the Law of Contracts, §4 above), liability for damages is an important remedy in case of delay, defective performance or other breaches of contract. There is no act in Finland that provides general provisions for contractual liability for damages. Such liability is instead regulated in acts applicable to specific contracts,[344] and many issues in connection with contractual liability for damages are to be solved on the basis of general principles of contract law. This is due to the fact that not all contracts are regulated in special acts. Moreover, not all special acts include provisions for liability for damages.[345]

362. The aggrieved party is usually to be compensated with a sum that will put him as nearly as possible into the hypothetical position he would have been in had the contract been duly performed, that is in accordance with the 'positive interest' (in Finnish: *positiivinen sopimusetu*). Another, more limited, way to be compensated is in accordance with a hypothetical situation in which no preparations for contract formation has taken place, that is in accordance with the 'negative interest'

---

340. This general act is thus subject to provisions on limitations that are found in special legislation (s. 2).
341. *See also* Norros II 2012, 349–350. Stipulations on when the periods of limitation for different debts begin are found in ss 5–7, and based on s. 8, a general limitation period of ten years, starting from when the legal basis of the debt arose, will apply to other obligations than those covered by (the three-year limitation period of) ss 5–7.
342. Norros II 2012, 339–340.
343. Norros II 2012, 334–335.
344. Hemmo 1998, 28–29.
345. Saarnilehto et al. 2012, 499.

(in Finnish: *negatiivinen sopimusetu*). Although the Finnish system for compensation is of German origin, the first possibility can be said to correspond to the English so-called expectation interest and the second to the so-called reliance interest.[346]

363. Negligence (culpa) is the main rule, not only for delictual liability for damages but for contractual liability for damages as well. However, in case of contractual liability for damages, the reversed burden of proof is the norm. In other words, although negligence is the basis for liability, the existence of a breach of contract in itself indicates that the party in breach has acted negligently. Thus, he is free from liability only if he proves that he has acted diligently or that he is not responsible for the event causing the loss.[347]

364. There are also other possibilities based on the law. For example, the Sale of Goods Act (355/1987) distinguishes between liability for direct loss and liability for indirect loss due to breach of contract. The damages for direct loss are based on the so-called principle of control liability. The said principle entails that liability for loss arises unless it is shown that the event that caused the loss has not been within the party's sphere of control. This can be illustrated with section 27(1) of the act in question that deals with the seller's control liability in case of delay. It states: 'The buyer is entitled to damages for losses that he suffers because of the seller's delay in delivery, unless the seller proves that the delay was due to an impediment beyond his control which he could not reasonably be expected to have taken into account at the time of the conclusion of the contract and whose consequences he could not reasonably have avoided or overcome.'[348]

365. Liability for indirect loss is based on negligence. This is made clear in section 27(4) of the Sale of Goods Act, which states: 'The buyer is always entitled to damages, including indirect losses, if the delay or loss is due to negligence attributable to the seller.' In connection herewith, section 70(1) of the Sale of Goods Act on the mitigation of loss is to be noted as well. It states: 'The injured party must take reasonable measures to mitigate his loss.' An injured party that fails to do so is to bear the corresponding part of the loss himself. It is moreover possible to adjust the amount of damages based on section 70(2) of the Sale of Goods Act, which states: 'The amount of damages payable to the injured party may be adjusted if the amount is unreasonable taking into account the possibilities of the breaching party to foresee and prevent the loss as well as other circumstances.'

---

346. Hemmo 1998, 148–149, Hemmo II 2003, 260–261.
347. Mononen 2004, 1389.
348. *See also* s. 40(1) on the seller's control liability for losses that the buyer suffers because of a defect in the goods.

366. In some situations, strict liability is applied. This means that a person is legally responsible for the damage and loss caused by his acts and omissions regardless of negligence.[349] In addition, liability without exception (in Finnish: *poikkeukseton vastuu*) is a possibility. This means that liability is not exempted even in case of force majeure and similar (as in strict liability).[350]

367. Chapter 5, section 20(1) of the Consumer Protection Act (38/1978, as amended 16/1994) on the seller's liability for the consumer's direct loss in case of a defect in the goods can be mentioned as an example of liability without exception. This section states: 'The buyer shall be entitled to compensation for loss that he/she suffers because of a defect in the goods.' However, based on this same section, liability for the consumer's indirect loss in case of a defect in the goods requires negligence.

368. The impact of a warranty given by the seller is to be also noted. Liability for damages in case of a warranty does not presuppose argumentation based on seller's negligence; instead, liability can in these cases be based directly on the fact that such a warranty has been given.[351] This is made clear in section 40(3) of the Sale of Goods Act, which states: 'The buyer is always entitled to damages, including indirect losses, if the defect or loss is due to negligence attributable to the seller or if the goods did not, at the time of the conclusion of the contract, conform to an express warranty of the seller.'

369. Especially in the case of B2B contracts, freedom of contract is an important principle.[352] It is, for instance, common to include a penalty clause/a clause on liquidated damages in such contracts, where the (amount of) actual damage is difficult to ascertain. The clause provides for payment of a beforehand agreed upon sum in case of breach of contract. Consequently, there is no need for the injured party to prove the actual damage caused by the breach, and it is quite possible that the party in breach will pay more than the damage he caused. The party in breach cannot avoid payment by providing proof of the fact that the breach did not cause any damage. As a starting point, it is also irrelevant whether the party in breach has acted negligently or not (*see also* Chapter 3, §1, IV above).[353]

370. Contracts often include different kinds of limitation of liability clauses; it is very common to limit a party's liability for indirect loss. Exemption clauses/ limitation of liability clauses, which limit or exclude a party from liability, can be in the form of standard terms or in the form of individually negotiated terms.[354] These clauses change the normal risk allocation between the contracting parties. As a starting point, they are nonetheless legally binding. According to Supreme Court

---

349. Mononen 2004, 1380.
350. Hemmo 1998, 39–41.
351. Wilhelmsson et al. 2006, 140.
352. Mononen 2004, 1381, 1388–1389.
353. Hemmo II 2003, 335–337, Hemmo 2005, 311, Hemmo 2008, 504–505, Lindfelt 2011, 204, Sund-Norrgård II 2015, 128.
354. *See* Sund-Norrgård II 2015, 128–140 for examples of different limitation of liability clauses.

decision KKO 2012:72, this is true also when the exemption clause/limitation of liability clause is comprehensive, provided that it is sufficiently clear and unambiguous. Certainly, it is possible that section 36 of the Contracts Act (228/1929, as amended 956/1982) is applicable in some situations, and limitation of liability clauses have in fact traditionally been seen as a type of clause that typically will be adjusted in court.[355]

371. It should be especially noted that a party's liability cannot, as a main rule, be limited in case he is guilty of gross negligence.[356] This is a form of negligence that can be placed between 'normal' negligence and intent, nonetheless closer to intent. Based on legal writing, gross negligence may be at hand when a party shows indifference, essentially diverges from the standard of care applicable to a given situation, neglects to undertake measures of precaution needed in order to avoid vast damage, or starts doing a job that requires qualifications that he clearly does not have. A highly qualified person who does not act in accordance with the 'norm' of the field in question is also more easily considered gross negligent than an unqualified non-specialist.[357]

372. Unclear exemption clauses are to be interpreted to the detriment of their drafter (*in dubio contra stipulatorem*), and exemption clauses are also to be interpreted narrowly. According to Supreme Court decision KKO 1992:178, this is especially so if the clause in question is drafted by only one of the parties and has a general, unclear content. In addition, an exemption clause can be 'surprising and burdensome' from the point of view of the other party, wherefore his attention must be especially drawn to it in order for it to become binding upon him. This is typically the case if the clause essentially diminishes the party's rights or increases his responsibilities in comparison to non-mandatory law or, where no such law exists, general principles of contract law or usage within the field.[358]

373. Naturally, an exemption clause in a B2C contract that restricts the consumer's right to damages shall be invalid if it is contrary to mandatory provisions of the Consumer Protection Act (*see also* Chapter 3, §1, III above).

---

355. Government bill 247/1981, 15, Saarnilehto 2009, 176.
356. For information on the discussion (in Sweden) concerning whether this is a correct approach, or whether the problem should be solved solely on the basis of s. 36 of the Contracts Act, *see* Sund-Norrgård II 2015, 124–127 and references.
357. Taxell 1972, 101, Hemmo II 2003, 288, Saarnilehto 2005, 7, Liebkind 2009, 136–137, 140–144, Sund-Norrgård II 2015, 126.
358. Sund-Norrgård II 2015, 127 and references.

§8. RESTITUTION

374. Following contract termination, the situation should, where possible, be restored as it was before the contract was concluded.[359] Issues like these were discussed already above (*see* §3 of this Chapter 6) and will, for this reason, not be discussed here again. However, the illuminating section 64 of the Sale of Goods Act (355/1987) can be mentioned once more. It states: 'Avoidance of the contract releases the seller from his obligation to hand over the goods and the buyer from his obligation to pay the price and to take delivery', and '[i]nsofar as the contract has been performed, each party is entitled to claim restitution from the other party of whatever the latter party has received'.

375. It can also be pointed out again that since it may be impossible to restore the situation as it was before contract conclusion, long-term contracts are treated as having full legal effect up until termination.[360]

---

359. Taxell 1972, 201 and Supreme Court decision 1984 II 198.
360. Taxell 1972, 203–204.

Part II. Specific Contracts

Chapter 1. Agency (Commercial Representatives)

376. The Act on Commercial Representatives and Salesmen (417/992, hereinafter 'the Agency Act') is an act implementing the Directive for the coordination of the laws of the Member States relating to self-employed commercial agents (86/653/EEC). It was prepared as a Nordic legislative collaboration, and the Finnish legislator articulated the importance of striving towards legislative similarities in the Nordic countries on the subject matter.[361]

377. According to section 1 of the Agency Act, a so-called representation contract is concluded between a commercial representative – or an agent, which is the term I hereinafter use (in Finnish: *kauppaedustaja*), and a principal (in Finnish: *päämies*), where the agent 'has undertaken continuously to promote the sale or purchase of goods on behalf of the principal by obtaining offers for the principal or by concluding sales or purchase contracts in the name of the principal'. The agent is thus an independent entrepreneur whose primary obligation is to promote the sale or purchase of goods on behalf of the principal and is not to be confused with an employee of the principal.

378. In the Agency Act, the term 'salesman' is used for a representative that in fact is an employee of the principal.[362] Salesmen are not discussed further.

379. It can also be noted that distributors act as independent contractors on their own behalf; they are not agents/middlemen and are not covered by the Agency Act.

380. The Agency Act is, in accordance with section 2, non-mandatory legislation, albeit with some exceptions that are specifically mentioned in the act. Due to the fact that the agent usually is economically weaker than the principal and thereby presumably in need of protection, the legislator found reason to include some mandatory provisions in the Agency Act.[363] Most provisions of the Agency Act nevertheless 'apply only unless otherwise provided in the contract, in the practice adopted by the parties or the trade, or in other usage which is to be deemed binding on the parties' (section 2(1)).

---

361. Government bill 201/1991.
362. *Ibid.*
363. *Ibid.*

381. The Agency Act does not include any mandatory provisions on the formation of agency contracts. An agency contract thus may, for instance, be oral.[364] However, according to section 3 of the act, 'the contract and any amendments thereto shall be concluded in writing' if either party requests it. This is a mandatory provision; a contract term that restricts this right of a party 'shall be null and void'. According to preparatory legislative work of the Agency Act, the said demand for written form is to be considered satisfied when the content of the contract appears from one or several documents or, for example, from the correspondence between the parties.[365]

382. Merely a position as an agent does not establish the competence to conclude contracts on behalf of the principal. To the contrary, as a main rule, an agent 'may conclude agreements on behalf of the principal only under specific authorization' (section 32(1)). Despite this, an agreement will in some cases be considered binding on the principal also without a specific authorization. This is so for example, if the principal has given the agent such forms that bear the name of the principal and which, after being completed by the agent, can be deemed to be intended as proof of a contract formed on behalf of the principal (section 32(2)). Such a form thus has a similar effect as a traditional power of attorney.[366]

383. It is to be observed that competency to conclude contracts that are binding on the principal does not in itself mean that the agent is 'entitled to collect payment for the goods sold, or, after the conclusion of the contract, to grant an extension for payment or a price discount, or otherwise to alter the contract' (section 37(1)).

384. In situations where a contract has been concluded through the contribution of the agent, or in his geographical area/among a group of clients entrusted to him, he may receive a notice regarding a defect or deficiency in the goods or a delay in their delivery and the like on behalf of the principal. This competency to receive notes does, however, not give the agent a right to 'make decisions regarding such notice even if he were entitled to conclude contracts binding on the principal' (section 38).

385. From the point of view of a third party that has concluded a contract with the agent, the Agency Act protects his trust in the actions of the agent more extensively than the general provisions of the Contracts Act (228/1929).[367] For instance, section 33 of the Agency Act requires the principal to notify a third party of his unwillingness to accept a contract concluded by the agent even in a situation where

364. Telaranta 1993, 18.
365. Government bill 201/1991.
366. Hemmo I 2003, 551.
367. Hemmo I 2003, 552–553.

the agent has concluded it without authorization or exceeding his competence. If the principal fails to do so without undue delay after learning about the contract, he is deemed to have accepted the contract.[368]

386. Section 34 of the Agency Act requires a principal that does not want to accept an offer received by the agent to, without undue delay after receiving the offer or after learning of the contents of the offer, notify the offeror thereof. Also, in this case a principal who fails to act in accordance with the provision – that is, remains passive – is considered to have accepted the offer.[369]

387. An agency contract is usually a long-term cooperational relationship where inter-party trust is important[370] and where the principle of loyalty has an impact as well. These issues will be discussed next. For instance, section 5(1) of the Agency Act obliges an agent, in performing his activities, to 'look after the interests of the principal, act dutifully and in good faith towards him as well as comply with any reasonable instructions given by the principal'. Since the principle of loyalty is regulated in such general terms, its more specific content will be specified in each case based on the contract, the practice adopted by the parties or the trade, and other circumstances of the case.[371] In Supreme Court decision KKO 2020:96, the court found that an agent had acted contrary to the principle of loyalty in a situation where the agent – shortly after the agency contract had been terminated by the principal – had presented a machine that competed with the principal's machine. The agent had developed and manufactured it during the term of the agency contract using technical solutions that were protected by the principal's utility model.

388. It can be specifically observed that although actions that lead to an economic loss for the principal can be seen hardly as complying with the principle of loyalty, section 6 of the Agency Act gives the agent the right to accept tasks also from other persons besides the principal, as long as this is not contrary to his obligation under section 5(1). It is nevertheless possible to include a non-compete clause in the agency contract,[372] and it may even be possible to argue that an obligation not to compete with the principal could be based on the principle of loyalty only.[373]

389. The agent has, based on section 5(2) of the Agency Act, an obligation to inform the principal of any circumstances that may be of relevance in performing

---

368. According to s. 19 of the Contracts Act such a duty to inform a third party may be required in situations, where the principal has 'special reason to believe' that the agent will enter into a transaction with a third party in good faith although the authorization has been revoked.
369. According to Ch. 1 of the Contracts Act an offer is usually deemed rejected if the offeree remains passive; as a main rule there is no obligation for him to provide an answer to the offer if he does not want to conclude a binding contract. *See also* Hemmo I 2003, 552.
370. Hemmo I 2003, 553.
371. Viljakainen 2004, 65, Sund-Norrgård 2011, 65.
372. Here s. 31 of the Agency Act, which concerns agreements restricting the activities of an agent following the termination of the agency contract is to be observed.
373. Sund-Norrgård 2011, 66 and references.

his activities. This duty to inform concerns, in particular, any offers that the principal might accept, as well as contracts that the agent has concluded on behalf of the principal.

390.   Section 7 of the Agency Act (as amended 646/2018) concerns the agent's obligation to maintain secrecy. According to it an agent, during the period of validity of the agency contract as well as thereafter, shall not make use of or disclose to third parties trade secrets of the principal in case he thereby 'would be acting in violation of good business practice'.

391.   Although the Agency Act does not regulate the principal's obligation not to disclose the agent's business secrets, such an obligation may follow on the basis of section 8 of the Agency Act.[374] According to section 8(1) of the Agency Act, a principal 'shall act dutifully and in good faith' towards the agent which, for instance, means that a principal has an obligation to support the agent. This obligation was considered so obvious that no specific provision on the same was included in the Agency Act.[375] The other paragraphs of section 8 concern the principal's information duty towards the agent. For instance, according to section 8(2), the principal is to provide the agent 'with all the information necessary for the performance of his activities and provide him with the necessary material, such as samples, models, specifications and price-lists'.

392.   An agent is entitled to payment in the form of a commission. The right to commission on a transaction concluded during the period of validity of the agency contract is regulated in section 10. A commission is, as a rule, to be paid if the transaction is concluded with the contribution of the agent or the transaction is concluded with a third party that belongs to the area or group of clients which has especially been entrusted to the agent. Under certain conditions, an agent is also, based on section 11, entitled to a commission although the transaction is concluded after the termination of the agency contract.

393.   If the agent has brought the principal new clients or significantly increased the volume of business with existing clients, in situations where the principal continues to gain substantial profit from business with such clients, the agent may be entitled to a separate indemnity from the principal upon the termination of the contract. The prerequisites for such a right are regulated in section 28 of the Agency Act.

394.   The need to protect the weaker party, that is the agent, is visible also from the mandatory section 23 on termination of an agency contract that is valid for the time being. This provision, as well as section 25 on the right of a party to cancel the contract with immediate effect for an important reason, have similarities with the way in which these issues have been regulated in the Employment Contracts Act (55/2001).

---

374. Viljakainen 2004, 25–26.
375. Telaranta 1993, 47.

Chapter 2. Bailment

395. Bailment can be defined as transfer of possession of movable property/ chattel from one person, the bailor (in Finnish: *tallettaja*), to another person, the bailee (in Finnish: *talteenottaja*), for storage. In Finland, one can find rules on bailment in Chapter 12 of the Commercial Code (3/1734, as amended 390/1973).

396. Based on bailment, the ownership of the stored movable property is not transferred to the bailee. He may not sell it, and he is not either entitled to use the movable property unless otherwise agreed between the parties. Moreover, he shall take care of the movable property as if it was his own and return it to the bailor in the same condition as it was when it came into his possession. It is noteworthy that the bailee is obliged to return the same movable property that he got for storage; he may thus not choose to return another, albeit equally good chattel. Also, if the bailee handles the storage of the movable property against a fee (gratuitous bailment is equally possible), he must meet the standard of a careful person no matter how he normally handles his own affairs. It can also be observed that the bailor is entitled to get the stored movable property back from the bailee at any time.[376]

397. In case the movable property is lost or damaged, the bailee is liable to pay damages based on negligence (Chapter 12, section 2 of the Commercial Code).

398. If the storage of the movable property has caused the bailee necessary costs – for instance in the form of rent for storage room or similar – the bailor is liable for compensating the costs before the movable property is returned (Chapter 12, section 8 of the Commercial Code).

399. A typical example of bailment is when a customer leaves his coat, or other personal belongings, in the coatroom of a restaurant or a bar. The Consumer Disputes Board[377] has handled several cases related to bailment in customer service situations. In case 163/35/09 a customer, who had visited an art museum, had left his coat at a coat rack that was free of charge and unsupervised. Since the coat had gone missing, he claimed damages from the art museum. The Consumer Disputes Board was of the opinion that no compensation was to be awarded. It stated that the art museum is not responsible for personal belongings that a customer, by his own choice and free of charge, leaves at an unsupervised coat rack.

400. It can be observed that Chapter 8 of the Consumer Protection Act (38/ 1978, as amended 16/1994), which concerns certain consumer service contracts, does not apply to services consisting of the safekeeping of property of the consumer (section 1 of the said chapter). In other words, the rules of Chapter 12 of the Commercial Code also apply to such bailment.

---

376. Hoppu & Hoppu 2016, 198.
377. The Consumer Disputes Board is a neutral and independent expert body. The decisions of the Board are merely recommendations.

Chapter 3. Gaming and Wagering

401. Contracts with a purpose contrary to the law are invalid. Contracts with a purpose that is (only) contrary to good practice/moral are not forbidden by law, but since they are considered unwanted by society they are to be prevented as well. When talking about gaming and wagering, it is especially essential to notice that contracts on such redistribution of wealth that society wants to prevent are invalid. Illegal gambling is one example of this.[378]

402. Organized gambling, which for example means arranging gambling or keeping a room or other premises available for gambling is a crime based on Chapter 17, section 16(1) of the Criminal Code (39/1889, as amended 563/1998). According to section 16(2) of the said chapter, activities like pools, bingo, tote and betting games, money and goods lotteries and casino operations are covered by this provision. Although it may be difficult to draw the line between illegal gambling and such games that anyone can arrange without permission,[379] a game or activity is deemed to be gambling when winning is completely or partially dependent on chance or events beyond the control of the participants, and the possible loss is clearly disproportionate to the financial standing of at least one of the participants.

403. Based on rather old decisions of the Supreme Court, gambling debts cannot be successfully claimed in court proceedings. Also, in a case where the party that lost the bet has already paid his debt, the other party is not liable to return the payment.[380] Ämmälä discusses a more recent decision, which was awarded by the Helsinki Court of Appeal in 2000, where the parties had made a bet of EUR 5,000 on weight loss: one of them was to lose 20 kilograms over a short period of time, which he did. The claim that was based on the losing party's refusal to pay his debt was dismissed by the Court of Appeal on the grounds that the Finnish legal system does not protect this kind of debt, which is comparable to a gambling debt.[381]

---

378. Hemmo 2008, 239.
379. Government bill 6/1997, 137.
380. *See* for example Supreme Court decisions KKO 1931-II-139 and KKO 1946-II-308.
381. Ämmälä II 2000, 22.

Chapter 4. Sale of Goods

404. The Sale of Goods Act (355/1987) contains non-mandatory provisions on the sale of goods, which in the act is defined as 'sale of property other than real property' (section 1(1)). The non-mandatory nature of the act is evident from section 3. It states: 'The provisions of this Act are subject to the terms of the contract between the parties, to any practice which has been established between them and to any other usage which is to be considered binding on the parties.'

405. It is made clear in section 4 of the Sale of Goods Act that the provisions are subject to the provisions of the Consumer Protection Act (38/1978). Sales of consumer goods are regulated in Chapter 5 of the Consumer Protection Act (as amended 16/1994 and 1211/2013) which, to some extent, differs from the provisions of the Sale of Goods Act in order to adequately protect consumers.

406. In accordance with section 5 of the Sale of Goods Act, '[c]ertain international contracts for the sale of goods are governed by separate provisions'. The CISG entered into effect in Finland on 1 January 1989. In this regard, it is to be noted that Finland originally ratified it with the exception of Part II on the formation of contracts. Finland also made a declaration under Article 94 to the effect that the CISG does not apply to sales contracts where the parties have their places of business in Finland, Denmark, Iceland, Norway or Sweden.

407. On 1 June 2012, Finland became a party also to Part II of the CISG. This means that Finland nowadays applies both Part II (formation of contracts) and Part III (obligations of buyers and sellers), but contracts concluded between parties having their places of business in the Nordic countries are still excluded from the scope of application of the CISG.[382] The Sale of Goods Act is the result of a collaboration between the Nordic countries, and it is thus a rather logical choice to exclude contracts between parties from the Nordic countries from the scope of application of the CISG.

408. The Sale of Goods Act regulates the primary obligations of the contracting parties and the remedies for acting contrary to the contract but not, for example, the issue of contract formation. Provisions on contract formation through offer and acceptance are instead found in the Contracts Act (*see* Part I, Chapter 1, §1, I for a discussion on this issue). Also, other differences can be found between the CISG and the Sale of Goods Act. Many questions are nevertheless regulated in the same way since the CISG was observed in the drafting process of the Sale of Goods Act.[383] I will briefly address some of the differences below.

---

382. United Nations Information Service, Press Releases 22 May 2012, https://unis.unvienna.org/unis/en/pressrels/2012/unisl162.html, Sisula-Tulokas 2012, 5–6.
383. Sisula-Tulokas 2012, 3.

409. The Sale of Goods Act has a wider area of application than the CISG; for instance sales of shares, electricity and IPRs fall under the scope of the Sale of Goods Act.[384]

410. Unlike the CISG, the Sale of Goods Act is applicable to auctions, where second-hand goods, based on section 19, are considered sold 'as is'. It is to be observed that goods that are sold subject to an 'as is' clause or a similar general reservation concerning their quality are nevertheless to be considered defective if they do not conform with the (relevant) information given by the seller before the conclusion of the contract, or if the seller pre-contractually failed to disclose (relevant) facts about the goods, or if the goods are in essentially poorer condition than the buyer reasonably could expect based on the price and other circumstances.[385]

411. There is no provision on 'as is' clauses in the CISG, and neither does the CISG have a provision equivalent to section 18 of the Sale of Goods Act, which stipulates that goods are defective if they do not conform with such (relevant) information that the seller, or someone else on behalf of the seller, gave when marketing the goods.

412. In the Sale of Goods Act, one cannot find a provision equivalent to Article 42 of the CISG, according to which the delivered goods are to be 'free from any right or claim of a third party based on industrial property or other intellectual property'.

413. One cannot find an equivalence to Article 25 of the CISG, which defines fundamental breach, in the Sale of Goods Act.

414. According to section 54(4) of The Sale of Goods Act, the seller may not, as a main rule, declare the contract avoided because of delay in payment if the goods have already been handed over to the buyer. The CISG lacks such a stipulation.

415. A significant difference relates to the regulation of damages for breach of contract. Article 74 of the CISG focuses only on foreseeability (concerning all kinds of losses) in stipulating that a party's liability 'may not exceed the loss which the party in breach foresaw or ought to have foreseen at the time of the conclusion of the contract, in the light of the facts and matters of which he then knew or ought to have known, as a possible consequence of the breach of contract'. A party is exempted from liability in accordance with Article 79 due to an impediment beyond his control.

416. As has already been discussed above (*see* Introduction to the Law of Contracts, §4, and Part I, Chapter 6, §7), the Sale of Goods Act makes a distinction between direct and indirect losses, where the seller usually cannot avoid responsibility for direct losses. These kinds of losses can be defined as typical, foreseeable

---

384. Section 1 of the Sale of Goods Act, Wilhelmsson et al. 2006, 8.
385. *See also* Sund-Norrgård II 2015, 133–135 and references.

consequences of a breach of contract. Examples are costs for clearing up the situation in the form of phone bills and the like, costs for storage and transportation that have become redundant because of the delay, and additional costs for a cover purchase.[386] For instance, in case of a seller's delay in delivery, section 27(1) of the Sale of Goods Act releases him from liability for direct losses only if he proves that the delay was due to an impediment beyond his control.

417. Responsibility for indirect losses requires negligence: According to section 27(4) of the Sale of Goods Act '[t]he buyer is always entitled to damages, including indirect losses, if the delay or loss is due to negligence attributable to the seller'. Indirect losses are – non-exhaustively – specified in section 67. Examples of indirect losses are loss due to reduction or interruption in production or turnover and loss of profit arising because a contract with a third party has been lost or breached. Compared to direct losses the indirect losses are more difficult to foresee, for instance as to the extent of the damage caused.[387] It is not, however, always easy to make the distinction between direct and indirect losses. The issue has been discussed in several Supreme Court decisions over the years,[388] and some researchers consider the solution adopted is the CISG to be a simpler one that in practice can lead to more foreseeable, reliable results.[389]

418. Unlike the CISG, the Sale of Goods Act also includes a specific provision on adjustment of damages: According to section 70(2) '[t]he amount of damages payable to the injured party may be adjusted if the amount is unreasonable taking into account the possibilities of the breaching party to foresee and prevent the loss as well as other circumstances'.

419. It can be noted that some special legislation concerning the sale of goods also exists. One such example is the Housing Transactions Act (843/1994), which 'applies to the sale of housing shares or any other interest in a corporation conferring the right of possession to a residential apartment' (section 1, as amended 795/2005).

---

386. Wilhelmsson et al. 2006, 90.
387. Wilhelmsson et al. 2006, 94, Supreme Court decision KKO 1997:61.
388. *See*, for instance, Supreme Court decisions KKO 1997:61, KKO 2009:89, and KKO 2012:101.
389. Sandvik & Sisula-Tulokas 2013, 148–149.

Chapter 5. Building Contracts, Hire of Work and Skills

420. Contracts regarding hire of work and skills are service contracts. Based on such a contract, the principal (a customer, a client, etc.) entrusts a work performance to the service provider against payment of the agreed price. The service provider performs the work independently and should not be seen as an employee or an agent of the principal.

421. In Finland, there is no general legislation on service contracts or contracts regarding hire of work and skills. Specific service contracts are regulated in various acts, for example in Chapter 8 of the Consumer Protection Act (38/1978, as amended 16/1994, and 391/2002), and in the Act on Public Procurement and Concession Contracts (1397/2016).

422. There is no specific legislation in Finland on building contracts. One may find some notable provisions in, for example, the Land Use and Building Act (132/1999). According to section 119 of the said act (as amended 41/2014), '[a] party engaging in a building project shall ensure that the building is designed and constructed in accordance with building provisions and regulations and the permit granted'. Sections 117 and 117a–117l of the said act (as amended 958/2012, 1151/2016, 812/2017, and 927/2021) contain provisions on the minimum level for essential technical requirements, etc. More specific requirements of such kind are nonetheless usually included in the building contract and its appendices.[390]

423. It should be stressed that the building contract normally is a long-term cooperation contract, which also presupposes that the parties act in accordance with the principle of loyalty.[391]

424. Building contracts between a business (contractor) and a consumer (commissioner) are regulated in Chapter 9 of the Consumer Protection Act (38/1978, as amended 16/1994, 1258/2001 and 572/2020). The said chapter, dealing with the sale of building elements and construction contracts, contains detailed provisions on delivery, passing of risk, the contracting parties' liabilities and rights, as well as sanctions for breaches of contract. These provisions are mandatory in favour of the consumer; a contract term derogating from the same to the detriment of the consumer shall be void.

425. Building contracts, where both contracting parties are businesses, do not fall within the scope of the Sale of Goods Act (355/1987). This follows from section 2(1) of the act which states that it 'does not apply to a contract for the construction of a building or other fixed installation or structure on land or in water'.

---

390. Liuksiala & Stoor 2014, 17.
391. Rudanko 1989, 49.

However, some provisions of the Sale of Goods Act express general principles of contract law and may thus indirectly have an impact on building contracts as well.[392]

426. It is to be observed that the building contract is not an employment contract: The contractor normally takes upon himself – against a fixed fee to be paid by the developer (commissioner) – to complete a certain work result in the form of the construction or reparation of a building. The contractor is not performing this work under the developer's supervision and direction in return for pay, which is the definition of an employee. The building contract can instead be defined as a type of commission agreement.[393]

427. Contractual standard terms are generally important in the construction industry. At the moment, the General Conditions for Building Contracts formed in 1998 (YSE 1998) can be considered as the most important existing set of standard terms. YSE 1998 were drawn up in collaboration with three central confederations and endorsed by The Finnish Association of Building Owners and Construction Clients. They apply to building contracts between business operators and include detailed, but presumably balanced, provisions on content, scope and period of a building contract, liabilities of the contracting parties, surety and insurance, obligation to pay, plan modifications and price changes, title and risk, organization, meetings and proceedings, termination and transfer of a building contract as well as disagreements and their resolution.

428. YSE 1998 normally become part of a particular building contract through an express reference to the terms. Due to the fact that YSE 1998 is a set of terms largely used in the field, it is nonetheless possible that they have an impact also in those cases where no direct reference to them is made in the building contract. This follows from the fact that they might be considered customary law.[394]

429. There are also other standard terms used in the construction industry, and for example Ryynänen is of the firm opinion that YSE 1998 are not – at least not in their entirety – to be considered customary law.[395] A reference can also be made here to Supreme Court decision KKO 2007:41 focusing on the previous standard terms YSE 1983. The Supreme Court stresses in this decision the need for parties to actually agree on the application of YSE 1983 in order for them to become binding. It may be noted that in the case of any conflict in the content, the contract as well as the minutes of the building contract negotiations precede YSE 1998 in the order of validity of contract documents.[396]

---

392. Ryynänen 2016, 7–10. *See also* Ryynänen 2019 for a discussion on the interpretation of YSE 1998.
393. Section 1 of the Employment Contracts Act (55/2001). *See also* Halila & Hemmo 2008, 48–49.
394. Halila & Hemmo 2008, 53.
395. Ryynänen 2016, 10.
396. Section 13 of YSE 1998.

430. Construction disputes often seem to concern additional work or modifications. For instance, the contractor's right to receive compensation for additional work or modifications was the subject of Supreme Court decisions KKO 2007:5, KKO 2008:19, and KKO 2018:13, and 75 out of 234 construction disputes decided in the courts of appeal during the time period 1994–2012 concerned additional work or modifications as well.[397]

---

397. Ryynänen 2013, 874. It can be noted that in, for instance, Supreme Court decisions KKO 2014:26, KKO 2016:79, KKO 2017:14, KKO 2019:73, and KKO 2019:88 the disputes concerned other issues in connection with YSE 1998.

Chapter 6. Lease: Commercial and Agricultural Leases

431. With a contract of lease, the lessor gives the right to use an object to the lessee for a specific period of time, or until further notice, against compensation, usually in the form of rent payable in money. The object of the contract of lease may be a building, a part of a building, real property or movable property. There are several – rather detailed – acts in Finland on different kinds of leases.[398] There are nevertheless not many Finnish provisions applicable to leases of movable property, such as a car or a machine, and in practice these situations are resolved on the basis of general contract law rules and principles. It may thus be a good idea to agree on the rights and obligations of the parties in the contract document.[399]

432. The Act on Residential Leases (481/1995) applies to 'any agreement (residential lease agreement) by which a building or any part thereof (apartment) is leased to another person for residential purposes'. Under such a contract of lease, a plot of land may also be assigned for use in conjunction with an apartment. The act moreover applies 'to shared access facilities or equipment located on the property or in the building, to which the tenant has access' (section 1).

433. The Act on Residential Leases does not apply to the operations of lodging establishments (section 2), even though a hotel room certainly is used by the guest in a similar fashion as required in section 1. It can be specifically noted that the Act on Commercial Leases (482/1995) is not applicable to lodging either, due to the fact that a hotel room or the like is used for (temporary) residence by the lessee.[400]

434. The Act on Commercial Leases is applied when a building or any part thereof (apartment) is used for any other purpose than residence, in other words as business premises. Also, under this kind of a contract of lease, a plot of land may be assigned for use in conjunction with the business premises, and the act applies to shared access facilities or equipment located on the property or in the building, to which the tenant has access (section 1).

435. It is clearly stated in section 1 of both these acts that the use of an apartment will be determined on the basis of the agreed principal use for it. In other words, the Act on Residential Leases is applicable when the apartment is used as residence, and the Act on Commercial Leases is applicable in other cases, for instance when it is used as a warehouse, a shop, a garage, or as a factory.

436. The provisions of both acts are non-mandatory unless otherwise provided in the act, or in case derogations from them are otherwise to be considered prohibited (section 3 of the Act on Residential Leases and section 2 of the Act on Commercial Leases). In reality, there is more room for freedom of contract in cases

---

398. Saarnilehto et al. 2012, 1075–1076.
399. Saarnilehto et al. 2012, 1080–1081.
400. Saarnilehto et al. 2012, 1077.

where the Act on Commercial Leases applies; there are considerably more mandatory provisions included in the Act on Residential Leases in order to protect the weaker lessee.[401] For instance according to section 52 of the Act on Residential Leases, the required period of notice is considerably longer when the lessor terminates the agreement than when the lessee terminates it. A contract clause that reduces the lessor's notice period, or extends the lessee's notice period, is null and void. For contracts that fall under the scope of the Act on Commercial leases, the situation is different. Section 42 that regulates notice periods is non-mandatory. The parties may thus agree otherwise on this issue.

437. When the leased object is a real estate or a plot of land, the Land Tenancy Act (258/1966) is applicable to the contract. The act includes general provisions (in Chapter 1), which are applicable to all contracts of land lease, as well as special provisions on five different types of land leases, which will not be discussed further.

438. Contrary to the Act on Residential Leases and the Act on Commercial Leases, the Land Tenancy Act is not to be applied to a contract of lease under which a building or a part thereof is leased in such a manner that a plot of land is also assigned for use in conjunction with the apartment (section 88, as amended 655/1987). In other words, when it is possible to apply the provisions on residential or commercial leases, the Land Tenancy Act shall not be applied. For instance in decision 29 March 2006 (S 05/1672) of the Turku Court of Appeal, the court stated that the Act on Commercial Leases should be applied to the lease contract instead of the Land Tenancy Act since the lessee had used the warehouse, while the leased plot of land was mainly not in use.[402]

439. It can be observed that separate provisions or regulations apply to official residences of the state, a municipality or some other public corporation. This is made clear in section 2 of the Act on Residential Leases.

440. In case of residential and commercial leases, the contracts of lease and amendments thereto are to be made in writing. This is required by section 5 of the Act on Residential Leases and section 4 of the Act on Commercial Leases. If the contracting parties do not comply with this requirement, the contract is still valid, but it is considered as being in force until further notice. Consequently, parties that wish to conclude a contract of lease for a specific period of time must do so in writing.

441. A contract of land lease is to be made in writing and both contracting parties shall sign it (there are some exceptions to this requirement, which will not be discussed here). A term in a contract of land lease that is not included in the written contract document is considered to be invalid (section 3 of the Land Tenancy Act).

---

401. *Ibid.*
402. This decision is discussed in Saarnilehto 2006, 8–10.

There are some other mandatory provisions in this rather detailed act as well. Nonetheless, also in the case of land lease, the parties may agree rather freely on their rights and obligations in the contract of lease.[403]

442. As a main rule, a lessee is not allowed to transfer the leased object to a third party without permission from the lessor, and he is not allowed to sell it either (section 44 of the Act on Residential Leases, section 36 of the Act on Commercial Leases and section 6 of the Land Tenancy Act).

443. Possibilities to sub-lease parts of the apartment are regulated in section 17 of the Act on Residential Leases and in section 16 of the Act on Commercial Leases. Also some other provisions exist that diverge from the main rule forbidding transfers of the leased object.[404]

444. It can be noted that the lessee will nowadays be protected in a situation where the lessor, for example, sells the shares conferring possession of the leased apartment. In accordance with section 38 of the Act on Residential Leases, the contract of lease will be binding on the new owner if '1) the tenant has taken possession of the apartment before the assignment or transfer takes place; 2) the assignment contract contains a provision on the permanence of the lease agreement; or 3) a mortgage has been taken out to secure the lease'. This is equivalent to section 31 of the Act on Commercial Leases.[405]

---

403. Saarnilehto et al. 2012, 1080.
404. *See*, for example, Saarnilehto et al. 2012, 1086.
405. The lessee is protected also on the basis of s. 12 of the Land Tenancy Act (as amended 548/1995).

Chapter 7. Compromise Settlement

445. It may certainly be cheaper, faster, and otherwise wise, for parties to conflicts that might end up in general court, or a court of arbitration, to try to resolve those conflicts by mutual agreement on their own, with the assistance of their attorneys, or even through mediators.

446. So-called court mediation, which may be characterized as a combination of administration of justice and mediation,[406] is in Finland nowadays regulated in the Act on mediation in civil matters and confirmation of settlements in general courts (394/2011). The act applies, according to section 1, to mediation in civil matters and contested petitionary matters in general courts (court mediation). The objective of court mediation is, according to section 3 of the act, 'an amicable resolution of the matter', and a pre-condition for this proceeding is that 'the matter is amenable to mediation, and a settlement is appropriate in view of the claims of the parties'. In court mediation, the mediator is a judge in the court where the matter is pending (section 5), and appeal is prohibited in accordance with section 17.

447. It is to be observed that the act in question also provides for confirmation of enforceability of a settlement reached during out of court mediation. By out of court mediation is meant 'a structured process conducted on the basis of an agreement, rules or another similar arrangement and in which the parties to a civil matter voluntarily seek on their own to solve their conflict amicably with the assistance of a mediator' (section 18). In these cases, a decision on the confirmation of enforceability of the settlement is subject to appeal in accordance with section 24.

448. Among the organizations that provide mediation, the Finnish Bar Association can be mentioned. It offers a mediation procedure and has created mediation rules, which apply when the contracting parties have agreed that their disputes should be settled in accordance with this procedure.[407] Also FAI, which is a part of the Finland Chamber of Commerce, administers mediations under the Mediation Rules of the Finland Chamber of Commerce. It can be observed that the settlement may be confirmed in an arbitral award in accordance with section 12 of these Mediation Rules, which were launched on 1 June 2016.[408]

---

406. Knuts 2006, 6, Sund-Norrgård 2013, 333.
407. The mediation rules as well as information on the procedure can be found on the website of the Finnish Bar Association www.asianajajaliitto.fi. The association has also drafted a model mediation agreement and mediation clause, which are available on the website.
408. The Finland Arbitration Institute, Mediation Rules, http://arbitration.fi/mediation/mediation_rules/.

Chapter 8. Suretyship

449. According to section 2 of the Act on Guaranties and Third-Party Pledges (361/1999), a guaranty (in Finnish: *takaus*) is 'a commitment by which the undertaking party (guarantor) promises to answer for the repayment of another person's (debtor) obligation (principal debt) to a creditor'. This section defines a secondary guaranty (in Finnish: *toissijainen takaus*) as 'a guaranty where the guarantor is liable for the principal debt only if the debtor fails to repay', while a surety (in Finnish: *omavelkainen takaus*) is 'a guaranty where the guarantor is liable for the principal debt as if it were the guarantor's own'. By general guaranty (in Finnish: *yleistakaus*) is meant 'a guaranty that covers also debts other than a specified principal debt'. There are also other definitions in this section that will not be addressed here.

450. The Act on Guaranties and Third-Party Pledges applies to guaranties and to pledges[409] for the debt of another person (section 1). It is thus logical that the guarantor's liability to the creditor lapses when the principal debt has been repaid or when it has otherwise lapsed (section 15(1)). A guaranty is a legal act for which there are no requirements as to form. It may thus be oral, albeit it normally is given in writing.[410]

451. The provisions of the Act on Guaranties and Third-Party Pledges are mainly non-mandatory. This is made clear in section 1(1) of the act, which states: 'If there is a provision contrary to this Act in another Act, the provision in the other Act prevails.' Moreover, the provisions of the Act on Guaranties and Third-Party Pledges apply, based on section 1(2) if it 'has not been otherwise provided in the undertaking on the guaranty or pledge, in the practice between the parties, in commercial custom, or in another custom binding on the parties'.

452. In the event that the undertaking is given by a private guarantor (which, in section 2(6) is defined as a natural person giving a guaranty) or pledgor to a lender (which, in section 2(7) is defined as a business, or a person pursuing a business, who in the pursuit of the business issues credit or security against a guaranty or other security), the provisions of the Act on Guaranties and Third-Party Pledges are, based on section 1(3), 'mandatory in the favour of the guarantor or pledgor'.

453. The guaranty is considered to have been given as (merely) a secondary guaranty unless it has been given as a surety, or it has been otherwise agreed on the contents of the guaranty (section 3(1)). In case of a secondary guaranty, the guarantor is responsible for the debt only if the debtor fails to pay it. The creditor can thus demand payment of the guarantor only after he has tried to collect the debt from the debtor first, and the debtor has been found insolvent as required in the act. In case of a surety, the guarantor is liable for the principal debt as if it were his own.

---

409. Pledges are discussed below in Ch. 9.
410. Saarnilehto et al. 2012, 1224–1225, Hoppu & Hoppu 2016, 249.

The creditor may thus claim performance directly from the guarantor as soon as the debt has become due and the debtor has neglected to pay it.[411]

454. When several guaranties have been given for the same principal debt, the presumption, that is if nothing else is agreed, is that each individual guarantor 'is liable to the creditor for the entire principal debt' (section 3(3)).

455. In case the guaranty is to cover also interest or other incidental costs, this has to be agreed upon. Otherwise, a guaranty is 'deemed to have been given only for the principal amount of the principal debt' (section 4(1)). Based on section 5(1), it is also required that a general guaranty indicates 'the monetary upper limit of the guarantor's liability, as well as the period of validity of the guaranty': This is, according to section 5(3) a mandatory provision in favour of the guarantor where the guarantor is a natural person.

456. Also, without any specific agreement on the issue, a guarantor is, based on section 28, entitled to recover from the debtor the amount of the principal debt that he has repaid to the creditor on the basis of the guaranty.[412]

457. Section 31 on the right of recourse against another guarantor is a non-mandatory provision. One may thus deviate from the same by agreement. Section 31(1) deals with the situation where guaranties for the same principal debt have been given simultaneously or subject to a requirement that other guaranties be given. In these cases, each guarantor – provided that no agreement on the mutual liability of the guarantors exists – 'has a right of recourse against the other guarantors, in proportion to the number of guarantors, for the amount of the principal debt that the guarantor has repaid'. He has a right to recourse for the amount paid that exceeds his share of the principal debt due and thereby has reduced the liability of the other guarantors.[413]

458. Section 31(2) deals with the situation, where several guaranties have been given independently and at different times. In these cases – also here provided that no agreement on the mutual liability of the guarantors exists – a guarantor has the right of recourse for the entire amount of the principal debt that he has repaid, but only against such guarantors who have given a prior guaranty.

459. If a guarantor has not paid on a claim under the right of recourse within a month of a demand to pay, or if he is insolvent, the guarantor who has repaid the debt has the right, based on section 31(3), to 'demand that all other guarantors pay their share of the unpaid claim under the right of recourse'.

---

411. Sections 21 (Dueness of a secondary guarantee) and 22 (Dueness of a surety) of the Act on Guaranties and Third-Party Pledges, Hoppu & Hoppu 2016, 249–250.
412. Hoppu & Hoppu 2016, 256.
413. Hoppu & Hoppu 2016, 257.

460. The guarantor's right of recourse from a security is regulated in section 30 and depends on who has given the security: Based on section 30(1), 'the guarantor has an equivalent right as that of the creditor to receive payment' for his claim 'from the security provided by the debtor for the principal debt'. This is logical since the debtor's security can be seen as given for the benefit of the creditor as well as the guarantor. In a situation where 'the security is given by someone else than the debtor', the guarantor is, based on section 30(3), entitled to recourse from the security only if there is an express agreement to this effect.

Chapter 9. Pledge

461. By way of introduction, it can be noted that in order for an asset to be usable as security under Finnish law, it is generally required that it can be individually identified, that it has monetary value and that it is freely transferable. Moreover, a valid underlying obligation is required since the right of pledge exists in order to secure repayment of debt.

462. Provisions on pledge are found in, for instance, Chapter 10 of the Commercial Code (3/1734, as amended 362/1999), and in the Act on Guaranties and Third-Party Pledges (361/1999). In section 2(8) of the latter act, third-party pledge is defined as 'an undertaking where the undertaking party (pledgor) hands over property (pledge) to the creditor as security for the repayment of the obligation of another person'. One may naturally also hand over property as security for one's own debt.

463. Special provisions on real estate liens are included in the Code on Real Estate (540/1995), and provisions on pledge are also included in the Bankruptcy Act (120/2004), as well as in several other acts that will not be discussed further.

464. In accordance with Chapter 10, section 1 of the Commercial Code, a pledge agreement should be concluded in the presence of two witnesses or in writing. This provision is, however non-mandatory, and there are no other mandatory provisions concerning the conclusion of a pledge agreement either. It may thus be concluded orally, albeit it is normally formed in writing.[414]

465. In order for the pledge to have the intended legal effect, an act of publicity is generally required. After the act of publicity, the right of pledge will be valid for instance in a situation where the ownership of the pledged object is transferred. In the case of movable property, the required act of publicity is fulfilled when possession of the object is transferred to the creditor or to a third person for safekeeping on behalf of the creditor. In case the object is in possession of a third party when the pledge agreement is formed, the right of pledge arises when the person in possession of the object is informed/notified of the existence of the pledge agreement.[415]

466. Sometimes, registration is needed. Shares of companies listed on the stock exchange can be mentioned as examples. Shares and the like are often used as security due to the fact that they may be valuable and are easy to hand over. But shares of companies listed on the stock exchange do not exist in physical form and thus cannot be transferred. The shares are instead listed in a book-entry account, and registration is needed in order for the right of pledge to arise: In accordance with section 6 of the Act on Book-Entry Accounts (827/1991, as amended 751/2012), the

---

414. Hoppu & Hoppu 2016, 258–259.
415. Hoppu & Hoppu 2016, 258–259.

entries registered in a book-entry account may include the pledge of a book entry, with the exception of a business facilities mortgage.

467. A pledgee is, based on Chapter 10, section 2 of the Commercial Code (as amended 687/1988) entitled to sell the pledge if the debt in question is due, the owner of the pledge has been informed about the fact that the object will be sold in case the debt is not paid within a certain period of time, and this time – which should be at least a month (sometimes two months) – has lapsed while the debt is still unpaid. According to Chapter 10, section 2(4) of the Commercial Code (as amended 752/2010), the interests of the owner of the pledge should be taken into account when the pledge is sold.

468. A pledgee is not allowed to use or lend the pledged object to others. This is made clear in Chapter 10, section 3 of the Commercial Code, which also states that the pledgee is to take due care of the object. The pledgee may, however, repledge the object as security for his own debt in accordance with the requirements of section 6 of the said chapter.

Chapter 10. Loans

469. A loan is usually described as a gratuitous right to use movable property/chattel, which is based on a personal contract between a lender (in Finnish: *lainananantaja*) and a borrower (in Finnish: *lainanottaja*). The fact that a loan is characterized as a personal contract means that the borrower is not entitled to transfer his right to a third party. The right also ceases in case of the borrower's death; it is not inherited by the borrower's successors.[416]

470. The right to usage based on a loan arises when the movable property is transferred to the borrower; a promise to lend is thus not considered to be binding. The gratuitousness of the loan distinguishes it from a lease.[417]

471. Even though the lender and the borrower may agree on a specific loan period, such an agreement is not necessarily binding in every situation. If the circumstances have changed unexpectedly and the change is somewhat significant, the lender is usually entitled to demand the chattel back. Also, if the borrowed chattel is sold 'the sale breaks the loan'. This means that the agreed loan period is not binding on the new owner. He may thus demand the movable property back.[418]

472. Based on Chapter 11, section 1 of the Commercial Code (3/1734), the borrower shall take good care of the borrowed movable property and return it to the lender in the same condition as it was when he received it. Tear due to normal usage is not considered to have damaged the chattel, but the borrower is usually responsible for the maintenance of the borrowed chattel.

473. According to Chapter 11, section 3 of Commercial Code, the borrower may nevertheless retain the chattel if he, with the lender's consent, for instance has put down necessary expenses on it. The borrower is only entitled to use the borrowed chattel as agreed and not for any other purposes.[419]

---

416. Saarnilehto et al. 2012, 1095, Hoppu & Hoppu 2016, 184.
417. *Ibid.*
418. Saarnilehto et al. 2012, 1095–1096.
419. Saarnilehto et al. 2012, 1096–1097.

Chapter 11. Contracts with the Government and Other Public Administrations

474. Private law deals with 'private matters', such as marriages or contracts, whereas the role of public law has traditionally been to act as the guarantor of private rights against public power. Nevertheless, public authorities in Finland also use contracts – instead of only administrative decisions – when implementing and executing legislation.

475. The main category of public contracts is the so-called administrative contract,[420] which in section 3(1) of the Administrative Procedure Act (434/2003) is defined as 'a contract, within the competence of an authority, on the performance of a public administrative task, or a contract relating to the exercise of public authority'. The act in question requires that when the administrative contract is formed, 'the fundamental principles of good administration shall be adhered to' and, moreover, 'the rights of the persons concerned shall be adequately protected', as shall 'their chances to affect the contents of the contract' in the drafting phase. In other words, the traditional idea of a need to protect private rights against the intrusion of public power is visible.

476. It should be noted that in case of a dispute concerning an administrative contract, it shall, in accordance with section 66 of the Administrative Procedure Act (as amended 854/2020) be considered as a matter of administrative litigation in an administrative court.

477. In case of administrative contracts, where the public authority acts in its public capacity, public law only is applicable. But public administrations certainly also, more frequently than before, use private contracts. In those cases where a public administration concludes a contract under private law, the contract is subject to private (contract) law. Such contracts are, for instance, employment contracts and rental contracts. Contracts of this kind concluded between a public body, for instance a municipality, and a private actor is thus basically treated in the same way as a contract formed between two private actors. However, when deciding to conclude or terminate such a contract, the public administration remains bound also by basic requirements of administrative procedural law, such as rules defining bias and objectivity.[421]

478. Sometimes the distinction between private contracts and administrative contracts is problematic. Mäenpää points out that this is especially so in the area of performing public tasks. Namely, in addition to such contracts that are purely private law contracts or clearly administrative by nature, there are contracts that

---

420. Mäenpää 2010, 657.
421. Mäenpää 2010, 657, 659.

'occupy a status in between public and private contracts' of which procurement contracts are examples.[422] The Supreme Court decision KKO 2013:19 can be noted in
this regard. A city and a company had concluded an outsourcing service contract
concerning viewing examinations to be performed in the health centre of the city.
The company demanded damages based on loss of income during the termination
period of the contract. The question that was to be solved by the Supreme Court was
whether the general courts that had tried the case had jurisdiction over the dispute
or whether the claim was based on an administrative contract and thereby ought to
be decided by an administrative court. The Supreme Court found that the content of
the contract was not linked to the exercising of public authority, but instead, it was
about the procurement of a service. It was thus not an administrative contract, and
the general courts had jurisdiction over the dispute.

479. Finland has undergone an extensive public procurement reform based on
the EU Directives on public procurement adopted in April 2014. An aim of the
reform is, for instance, to simplify procurement procedures. As of 1 January 2017,
the Act on Public Procurement and Concession Contracts (1397/2016) is in
force.[423] The provisions of this act will not be discussed further.

---

422. Mäenpää 2010, 658.
423. *See also* the information found at Ministry of Economic Affairs and Employment, Reform of Public Procurement Legislation, http://tem.fi/en/reform-of-public-procurement-legislation.

Chapter 12. Contract of Partnership

480. Provisions on the two types of partnerships that is general partnerships (in Finnish: *avoin yhtiö*) and limited partnerships (in Finnish: *kommandiittiyhtiö*) are found in the Partnerships Act (389/1988, as amended 1444/2015). The difference between the two types is that the partners – who can be either natural persons or organizations, such as other companies – of a general partnership are jointly and severally liable for the debts and other obligations of the partnership. Limited partnerships have one or several so-called limited partners (or silent partners), whose liability is limited to the amount of their capital investment. Based on Chapter 1, section 1 of the Partnerships Act, a limited partnership must have at least one general partner and at least one silent partner.

481. From the beginning of 2016, general partnerships and limited partnerships alike are formed through registration. In the past, they were both formed simply by the conclusion of a partnership agreement in free form; the registration had only a declarative purpose. Nowadays, Chapter 1, section 4 of the Partnerships Act provides for minimum requirements for the partnership agreement, which is to be formed in writing.

482. According to Chapter 1, section 2 of the Partnerships Act, a partnership must be reported for registration within three months from signing the partnership agreement. If not, the formation of the partnership expires (in accordance with section 3c). Based on the provisions on the entry into force of the amended act, which are included in Chapter 11, an unregistered partnership formed before 2016 must be reported for registration within two years from the start of 2016. Otherwise, the partnership will be dissolved. Since an unregistered partnership lacks legal capacity, the act includes provisions regulating actions with an unregistered partnership (Chapter 1, sections 3, 3a, 3b).

483. Besides the issue of formation of partnerships, the amendments to the act also relate to, for instance, the termination of partnerships and redemption of partnership interests. According to Government bill 17/2015, the overall purpose of the amendments to the act is to make the provisions on partnerships clearer in order to facilitate the usage of partnerships in situations where long-term investments are demanded, and foreseeability is needed.

Chapter 13. Quasi-Contracts

§1. *Negotiorum Gestio*

484. *Negotiorum gestio* refers to a situation in which a person, without proper authorization/power of attorney, voluntarily performs necessary legal acts or other measures on behalf of an absent or otherwise prevented person in order to protect his interests.[424]

485. A general provision on *negotiorum gestio* is found in Chapter 18, section 10 of the Commercial Code (3/1734). It provides for representation of an absent person in legal proceedings, but the provision has also been applied in situations other than court proceedings.

486. The principal is bound by the legal act performed on behalf of him if the conditions for *negotiorum gestio* are fulfilled. In this contemplation, the prerequisites of the said section of the Commercial Code may be useful. As a result, the principal should be away (travelling or the like) or otherwise prevented from acting himself: He should be both physically absent as well as not reachable by phone or similar. The person acting on behalf of the principal can, moreover, only act if he has no knowledge of anybody else acting on behalf of the principal with proper authorization. Finally, the situation should be so exceptional that it is necessary to quickly perform legal acts in order to avoid a significant damage. It should be mentioned that the conditions for *negotiorum gestio* usually prevail only for a short period of time.[425]

487. Chapter 18, section 5 of the Commercial Code states that a representative should receive a reasonable fee as well as a reimbursement of his costs. This section may, at least in some situations, be used as a legal basis also when contemplating these issues in case of *negotiorum gestio*.[426]

488. The person acting on behalf of the principal may become liable for damages towards the principal if the concluded contract is binding on the principal but does not meet the interests of the principal in the best possible way. Liability for damages towards the principal's contract party may occur in case the contract is not to be considered binding on the principal.[427]

§2. Enrichment Without Cause

489. Sometimes a person receives an economic benefit without acceptable legal grounds. A typical situation is when money payments are made by mistake to the

---

424. Hemmo 2008, 282.
425. Hemmo 2008, 284–285.
426. *See* the discussion in Hemmo 2008, 285–287.
427. Hemmo 2008, 286.

wrong person. Somebody thus receives an unjust enrichment at somebody else's expense. The legal remedy for these situations in the form of the doctrine of restitution of unjust enrichment, which according to Roman law was included in the concept quasi-contract, is also known in Finnish law.[428] The effects of unjustified performances may thus be eliminated in situations where contract law or tort law cannot be applied.

490. Since the prerequisites for restitution of unjust enrichment may be at hand in many different situations, there is no general provision or the like on this issue. Some scholars are of the opinion that restitution of unjust enrichment is a general principle of law, albeit with many exceptions. In any case, there are many norms – both specific provisions in the written law and unwritten, more generally applicable norms – that aim at eliminating the effects of unjustified performances.[429] The prerequisites for a general duty of restitution (not regulated by law) are that (1) there should be a profit or benefit (enrichment), which is (2) unjustified or unfounded, and (3) where the beneficiary profits at someone else's expense: There has to be a causal relationship between the profit and the loss. In principle, these prerequisites are clear, but in practice, problems may arise in their interpretation.[430]

§3. MONEY PAID BUT NOT DUE

491. 'Money paid but not due' may refer to several different situations. I will shortly address the situation where the debtor pays the debt to the wrong person, the situation where he pays it to the right person, but to a higher amount than required, and the situation where he pays it to the right person but prematurely.

492. If a person makes a money payment to another person by mistake – using the wrong account number or the like – the wrong payment is usually to be paid back based on restitution of unjust enrichment. This classical situation was mentioned already above.

493. The norm basis for restitution is a little trickier in case the payment to the right person is erroneous. Maybe it has been made twice, or otherwise to a higher amount than the actual debt. It is also here possible to base the duty of repayment on the general restitution of unjust enrichment. Another possibility would be to base it on *condictio indebity*, which is a principle with roots in Roman law. When applying *condictio indebity*, the actual circumstances of the case are considered to a larger extent: issues like the degree of negligence of the person making the payment, and the good faith of the receiver of the payment, may impact the outcome. According to Norros, *condictio indebity*, which in Sweden and the rest of the Nordic countries

---

428. Norros I 2012, 10 and references, Saarnilehto et al. 2012, 44.
429. Norros I 2012, 46–47.
430. Norros I 2012, 54–60.

probably would be used in these situations, is of little relevance in Finland. Usually, the doctrine of restitution of unjust enrichment will be used instead.[431]

494. There is also legislation applicable to these situations. Based on Chapter 9, section 13 of the Commercial Code (3/1734, as amended 390/1973), a miscalculation is not considered a payment, and in case such a mistake is noticed it should first be corrected, and thereafter the payment should be made in accordance with the correct calculation. Finnish courts appear to apply this provision without taking negligence and the like into consideration – in other words, *not* in accordance with *condictio indebity.*[432]

495. 'Money paid but not due' may also refer to a situation where a party pays his debt to the right person, but prematurely. The question to be answered is 'how early can he pay without the creditor having a right to refuse acceptance'? Usually, the parties are entitled to agree on the earliest moment when the obligation may be fulfilled. Typically, parties only agree on the latest possible time for performance. Such a contract term is normally interpreted as allowing the debtor to fulfil the obligation as early as he wishes. In other words, a debt is payable already before the due date: The amount of interest or other credit costs to be paid are nonetheless calculated on the basis of the original credit period.[433]

496. The Finnish legislation includes some provisions which specifically entitle the debtor to pay before the due date. One example is the regulation on the so-called consumer credit, which in Chapter 7, section 1(1) of the Consumer Protection Act (38/1978, as amended 861/2016) is defined as credit that a business, by agreement, grants or promises to the consumer in the form of, for instance, a loan. Based on Chapter 7, section 27 (as amended 746/2010), the consumer may pay his credit in total or in part before the due date. In such a case, the credit costs for the remaining unutilized credit time will be deducted.

---

431. Norros I 2012, 51–54.
432. Klami-Wetterstein 2014, 4–6.
433. Norros I 2012, 96–97.

Selected Bibliography

Books

Aarnio, Aulis. *Laintulkinnan teoria, Yleisen oikeustieteen oppikirja*. WSOY, 1989.
Aarnio, Aulis. *Oikeutta etsimässä. Erään matkan kuvaus*. Talentum, 2014.
Ämmälä, Tuula. 'Heikomman suoja'. In *Varallisuusoikeuden kantavat periaatteet*, edited by Ari Saarnilehto. WSOY, 2000: 97–109. *Ämmälä I 2000*.
Ämmälä, Tuula. *Sopimuksen pätemättömyyden korjaantumisesta*. Talentum, 1993.
Andersen, Mads Bryde & Eric Runesson. 'An Overview of Nordic Contract Law'. In *The Nordic Contracts Act*, edited by Torgny Håstad. Djøf Publishing, 2015: 15–41.
Annola, Vesa. *Sopimuksen dynaamisuus*. Turun yliopisto, 2003.
Bernitz, Ulf. *What Is Scandinavian Law? Concept, Characteristics, Future*. Stockholm Institute for Scandianvian Law, 1957–2010. Available online at http://www.scandinavianlaw.se/pdf/50-1.pdf.
Davies on Contract, edited by Upex, Robert & Bennett, Geoffrey. Sweet & Maxwell, 2004.
Gomard, Bernhard, et al. *Almindelig kontraksret*, 5. Udgave, Djøf Forlag, 2015. *Gomard et al. 2015*.
Grönfors, Kurt & Dotevall, Rolf. *Avtalslagen. En kommentar*, femte upplagan. Wolters Kluwer, 2016.
Grönfors, Kurt. *Avtal och omförhandling*. Nerenius & Santérus, 1995.
Haapio, Helena. *Next Generation Contracts: A Paradigm Shift*. Lexpert Ltd, 2013.
Halila, Heikki & Hemmo, Mika. *Sopimustyypit*. Talentum, 2008.
Hemmo, Mika. *Sopimus ja delikti*. Lakimiesliiton Kustannus, 1998.
Hemmo, Mika. *Sopimusoikeuden oppikirja*. Talentum, 2008.
Hemmo, Mika. *Sopimusoikeus I*. Talentum, 2003. *Hemmo I 2003*.
Hemmo, Mika. *Sopimusoikeus II*. Talentum, 2003. *Hemmo II 2003*.
Hemmo, Mika. *Vahingonkorvausoikeus*, 2. Painos. Sanoma Pro, 2005.
Hirvonen, Ari. *Mitkä metodit? Opas oikeustieteen metodologiaan*. Yleisen Oikeustieteen julkaisuja 17, 2011.
Hoppu, Esko & Hoppu Kari. *Kauppa- ja varallisuusoikeuden pääpiirteet*. Talentum Pro, 2016.
Husa, Jaakko. *The Constitution of Finland: A Contextual Analysis*. Hart Publishing, 2010.
Kaisto, Janne. *Esineoikeuden alkeet*. Forum Iuris, 2016.

Selected Bibliography

Kartio, Leena. 'Maakaaren ehdollisen kiinteistönsaannon sääntely – mietteitä eräiden reaktioiden johdosta'. In *Juhlajulkaisu Jarmo Tuomisto 1952 – 9/6 – 2012*, edited by Tero Iire. Turun yliopisto, 2012: 135–149.

Keskitalo, Petri. *From Assumptions to Risk Management. An Analysis of Risk Management for Changing Circumstances in Commercial Contracts, Especially in the Nordic Countries*. Kauppakaari Oyj, 2000.

Knuts, Gisela. *Förfarandegrantier vid domstolsanknuten medling*. Suomalainen Lakimiesyhdistys, 2006.

Koulu, Risto. *Kaupallisten riitojen sovittelu*. Edita Prima, 2006.

Koulu, Risto. *Välityssopimus välimiesmenettelyn perustana*. Edita, 2008.

Lindskog, Stefan. 'Jämkning i kommersiella avtalsförhållanden'. In *Aftaleloven 100 år, Baggrund, status, udfordringer, fremtid*, edited by Mads Bryde Andersen, et al. Djøf Forlag, 2015: 305–327.

Liuksiala, Aaro & Stoor Pia. *Rakennussopimukset*, 7. uusittu painos. Rakennustieto Oy, 2014.

Mäenpää, Olli. 'Finlande/Finland'. In *Des Contrats Publics – Comparative Law on Public Contracts*, edited by Rozen Noguellou & Ulrich Stelkens. Bruxelles: Bruylant, 2010: 657–673.

Mäenpää, Olli. *Hallinto-oikeus*. Sanoma Pro, 2013.

Mähönen, Jukka. 'Lojaliteettivelvollisuus ja tiedonantovelvollisuus'. In *Varallisuusoikeuden kantavat periaatteet*, edited by Ari Saarnilehto. WSOY, 2000: 129–143. *Mähönen II 2000*.

Mäkelä, Juha. *Sopimus ja erehdys. Sopimusoikeudellinen tutkimus oikeuserehdyksestä valinnanvapauden teorian näkökulmasta*. Suomalainen Lakimiesyhdistys, 2010.

Moilanen, Juha-Matti. *Sopimusten tulkintaperiaatteet*. Turun yliopisto, 1991.

Munukka, Jori. 'The Contractual Duty of Loyalty: Good Faith in the Performance and Enforcement of Contracts'. In *The Nordic Contracts Act*, edited by Torgny Håstad. Djøf Publishing 2015: 203–215.

Norros, Olli. *Inledning till obligationsrätten*. Forum Iuris, 2012. *Norros I 2012*.

Norros, Olli. *Johdatus velvoiteoikeuteen*. Forum Iuris, 2015.

Norros, Olli. *Velvoiteoikeus*. Sanoma Pro, 2012. *Norros II 2012*.

Nygren, Päivi. 'Sitoumusten kartoittaminen – välttämätön osa riskien hallintaa'. In *Ennakoiva sopiminen*, edited by Soile Pohjonen. WSOY Lakitieto, 2002: 215–240.

Nyström, Jan-Åke. *Kontraktsbrott vid agenturavtal*, Tredje upplagan. Norstedts Juridik Ab, 2004.

Ovaska, Risto. *Välimiesmenettely – kansallinen ja kansainvälinen riidanratkaisukeino*. Edita Publishing Oy, 2007.

Pöyhönen, Juha. *Sopimusoikeuden järjestelmä ja sopimusten sovittelu*. Suomalainen Lakimiesyhdistys, 1988.

Ramberg, Jan & Ramberg Christina. *Allmän avtalsrätt*. Tionde väsentligt omarbetade och utökade upplagan. Wolters Kluwer, 2016.

Rudanko, Matti. *Rakennuttajan myötävaikutushäiriöstä rakennusurakassa*. Suomalainen Lakimiesyhdistys, 1989.

Ryynänen, Juha. *Urakkasopimuksen muutokset*. Edita, 2016.

Saarnilehto, Ari, et al. *Varallisuusoikeus.* Sanoma Pro, 2012. *Saarnilehto* et al. *2012.*

Saarnilehto, Ari. *Sopimusoikeuden perusteet*, 7. uudistettu painos. Talentum, 2009.

Saxén, Hans. *Skadeståndsrätt.* Åbo Akademi, 1975.

Sisula-Tulokas, Lena. 'Skumma affärsmetoder, tvång och ohederlighet, HD 1997:67'. In *Avtalslagen 90 år, Aktuell nordisk rättspraxis*, edited by Boel Flodgren, et al. Norstedt Juridik AB, 2005: 317–328.

Sund-Norrgård, Petra. 'Draft Common Frame of Reference i finsk och svensk rättspraxis'. In *Isännän ääni – Juhlakirja Erkki Kustaa Rintala*, edited by Petteri Korhonen & Timo Saranpää, Talentum Pro, 2015: 525–544.

Sund-Norrgård, Petra. *Lojalitet i licensavtal.* Publications of IPR University Center & Juridiska föreningens publikationsserie, 2011.

Sund-Norrgård, Petra. *Tolkningen av franchiseavtal.* Forum Iuris, 2014.

Tammi-Salminen, Eva. *Sopimus, kompetenssi ja kolmas. Varallisuusoikeudellinen tutkimus negative pledge -lausekkeiden sivullissitovuudesta.* Suomalainen Lakimiesyhdistys, 2001.

Taxell, Lars Erik. *Avtal och rättsskydd.* Åbo Akademi, 1972.

Taxell, Lars Erik. *Avtalsrätt. Bakgrund, Sammanfattning, Utblick.* Juristförlaget, 1997.

Telaranta, K.A. *Kauppaedustaja, myyntimies ja yksinmyyjä.* Lakimiesliiton Kustannus, 1993.

Telaranta, K.A. *Sopimusoikeus.* Lakimiesliiton Kustannus, 1990.

Tepora, Jarno. *Inledning till grunderna för sakrätten.* Forum Iuris, 2009.

Tiitinen, Kari-Pekka & Kröger Tarja. *Työsopimusoikeus*, 6. uudistettu painos. Talentum, 2012.

Toiviainen, Heikki. *An Introduction to Finnish Business Law. A Comprehensive Survey of the Foundations and Main Rules of Finnish Corporate Law.* Edita Prima Oy, 2008.

Tuori, Kaarlo. *Rättens nivåer och dimensioner.* Forum Iuris, 2008.

Vihma, Väinö. *Vakuutuksenottajan tiedonantovelvollisuus vakuutussopimusta tehtäessä vakuutussopimuslain mukaan.* SVLY 8, 1945.

Viljakainen, Pentti. *Laki kauppaedustajista ja myyntimiehistä.* Myynnin ja markkinoinnin oikeusturva MOT, 2004.

Villa, Seppo, et al. *Yritysoikeus.* Talentum, 2014. *Villa* et al. *2014.*

von Bar, Christian & Eric Clive (ed.). *DCFR (Draft Common Frame of Reference).* Vol. 1, Full edn. sellier. European Law Publishers, 2009.

von Hertzen, Hannu. *Sopimusneuvottelut.* Suomen Lakimiesliiton kustannus, 1983.

Wilhelmsson, Thomas, et al. *Kauppalain pääkohdat.* Talentum, 2006. *Wilhelmsson* et al. *2006.*

Wilhelmsson, Thomas. 'Välityslausekkeen sovittelu elinkeinonharjoittajien välisessä suhteessa'. In *Juhlajulkaisu Esko Hoppu 1935 – 15/1 – 2005*, edited by Heikki Halila, Mika Hemmo & Lena Sisula-Tulokas. Suomalainen Lakimiesyhdistys, 2005: 411–423.

Wilhelmsson, Thomas. *Standardavtal och oskäliga avtalsvillkor.* Talentum, 2008.

Wuolijoki, Sakari. *Pankin neuvontavastuu. Varallisuusoikeudellinen tutkimus pankin neuvonta- ja tiedonantovelvollisuuksista.* Helsingin yliopisto, 2009.

Selected Bibliography

Articles and Legislative Preparatory Works

Ämmälä, Tuula. 'Lyhyesti hovioikeuksista'. *Oikeustieto* (6/2000): 21–24. *Ämmälä II 2000*.

Annola, Vesa. 'Sopimustulkinnan subjektiivisuus ja objektiivisuus'. *Edilex* (2012): 175–190.

Annola, Vesa. 'Yhteistoimintasopimuksen tulkinnan välineet'. *Oikeustieto* (6/2010): 4–8.

Edlund, Hans Henrik. 'Imbalance in Long-Term Commercial Contracts'. *European Review of Contract Law* 5, no. 4 (2009): 427–445.

Government bill 17/2015.

Government bill 201/1991.

Government bill 241/2006.

Government bill 247/1981.

Government bill 6/1997.

Halijoki, Juha. 'Oikeudenkäyntikulut ja niiden jakautuminen'. *Defensor Legis* (2/2000): 205–229.

Hoppu, Kari. 'Force majeure-tilanteiden tulkinnasta erityisesti COVID-19-taudin yhteydessä'. *Defensor Legis* (3/2020): 289–307.

Häyhä, Juha. 'Lojaliteettiperiaate ja sopimusoppi'. *Defensor Legis* (3/1996): 313–327.

Jokela, Heikki. 'Kestosopimusten sopeuttaminen muuttuneisiin olosuhteisiin'. *Defensor Legis* (1978): 133–171.

Kangas, Tanja. 'Privity of Contract in Financial Leasing'. *Edilex* (2009): 69–100.

Kartio, Leena. 'Esineoikeus valinkauhassa'. *Lakimies* (6–7/1998): 1057–1064.

Klami-Wetterstein, Paula. 'Virheellisen laskutuksen oikaisemisesta'. *Oikeustieto* (3/2014): 4–6.

Komiteanmietintö 1953:5.

Lagberedningens publikationer 1925 No. 2.

Lando, Ole. 'Nordisk formueret i Europæisk perspektiv'. *Tidskrift utgiven av Juridiska Föreningen i Finland* (6/2009): 753–761.

Liebkind, Anina. 'Limitation of Liability Clauses and Gross Negligence in Business-to-Business Contracts'. *Tidskrift utgiven av Juridiska Föreningen i Finland* (2/2009): 127–151.

Lindfelt, Villy. 'Sopimuksen päättyessä voimassa pysyvät sopimusmääräykset'. *Defensor Legis* (2/2011): 195–209.

Mäenpää, Kalle. 'Contract Negotiations and the Importance of Being Earnest'. *Tidskrift utgiven av Juridiska Föreningen i Finland* (4/2010): 322–350.

Mähönen, Jukka. 'Lojaliteettivelvollisuudesta toimeksiantosuhteessa'. *Oikeustieto* (5/2000): 10–11. *Mähönen I 2000*.

Mäkelä, Juha. 'Erehdysopillisia kehityssuuntauksia'. *Edilex* (2009): 95–117.

Mäkinen, Eija. 'Pysäköintivalvonta – julkista vai yksityistä?'. *Edilex* (2011): 1–23.

Mononen, Marko. 'Onko sopimusoikeudessamme yhtenäistä vastuuperustetta?'. *Lakimies* (7–8/2004): 1379–1397.

Muukkonen, P. J. 'Sopimusoikeuden yleinen lojaliteettiperiaate'. *Lakimies* (7/1993): 1030–1048.

Norros, Olli. 'Sopimusperusteiset muotovaatimukset'. *Lakimies* (2/2008): 183–211.

Ollila, Aki. 'Neuvottelulojaliteetti'. *Defensor Legis* (6/2016): 934–951.

Routamo, Eero. 'Kauppalain anti ostajapuolelle'. *Lakimies* (1988): 12–23.

Routamo, Eero. 'Vastaavuusteoria – viisaallekin kivinen?'. *Lakimies* (2/1980): 933–937.

Ryynänen, Juha. 'Urakkariidat hovioikeuksissa'. *Defensor Legis* (5/2013): 855–879.

Ryynänen, Juha. 'YSE 1998 ja sopimuksen tulkintasäännöt'. *Defensor Legis* (3/2019): 359–372.

Saarnilehto, Ari. 'Kommentoituja oikeustapauksia korkeimmasta oikeudesta, Välityslausekkeen kohtuuttomuus'. *Oikeustieto* (2/1997): 2–3.

Saarnilehto, Ari. 'Kommentoituja oikeustapauksia korkeimmasta oikeudesta, Välityslausekkeen sovittelu'. *Oikeustieto* (4/2003): 3–4.

Saarnilehto, Ari. 'Maanvuokra vai liikehuoneiston vuokra'. *Oikeustieto* (5/2006): 8–10.

Saarnilehto, Ari. 'Takaustarjous vai takaussitoumus?'. *Oikeustieto* (4/2009): 10–11.

Saarnilehto, Ari. 'Vastuun rajoitukset riskien hallinnassa ja vakioehdot'. *Edilex* (2005): 1–27.

Sandvik, Björn & Sisula-Tulokas Lena. 'HD 2012:101 – Ett nytt köplagsfall'. *Tidskrift utgiven av Juridiska Föreningen i Finland* (2/2013): 143–150.

Sisula-Tulokas, Lena. 'CISG pähkinänkuoressa'. University of Helsinki, 2012: 1–46, available online at https://docplayer.fi/29890128-Cisg-pahkinankuoressa.html. Visited on 9 March 2022.

Sisula-Tulokas, Lena. 'Handelssanktioner mot Ryssland och tillämpningen av CISG'. *Tidskrift utgiven av Juridiska Föreningen i Finland* (3/2015): 193–214.

Sisula-Tulokas, Lena. 'Kan en varas klimatbelastning vara ett köprättsligt fel?'. *Tidskrift utgiven av Juridiska Föreningen i Finland* (3/2020): 313–329.

Snyder, David V. 'The Case of Natural Obligations'. *Louisiana Law Review* 56, no. 2 (1996): 423–436.

SOU 1956:25.

Sullivan, Timothy J. 'The Concept of Benefit in the Law of Quasi-Contract'. *The Georgetown Law Journal* 64, no. 1 (October 1975): 1–26.

Sund-Norrgård, Petra, Antti Kolehmainen & Onerva-Aulikki Suhonen. 'The Principle of Loyalty and Flexibility in Contracts'. *Lapland Law Review* (2/2015): 190–208.

Sund-Norrgård, Petra. 'Friskrivningsklausuler i köpeavtal'. *Tidskrift utgiven av Juridiska Föreningen i Finland* (2/2015): 115–141.

Sund-Norrgård, Petra. 'Omförhandling och medling'. *Tidsskrift for Rettsvitenskap* (3/2013): 315–342.

Sund-Norrgård, Petra. 'The Interpretation of Licensing Agreements. Time for a Reassessment?'. *Nordiskt Immateriellt Rättsskydd* (3/2012): 235–247.

Sund-Norrgård, Petra. 'Värvningsklausuler i avtal mellan näringsidkare'. *Tidskrift utgiven av Juridiska Föreningen i Finland* (6/2016): 563–594.

Tammi-Salminen, Eva. 'Sopimus ja kolmas: velvoite- ja esineoikeutta yhdistävä vai erottava teema?'. *Edilex* (2010): 369–392.

Taxell, Lars Erik. 'Om lojalitet i avtalsförhållanden'. *Defensor Legis* (1–3/1977): 148–155.

Selected Bibliography

Vedenkannas, Matti. 'Avoimen innovaatioympäristön oikeudellisista rakenteista'. *Defensor Legis* (6/2009): 961–981.

Virtanen, Jenny. 'Todistustaakan ja vastuunrajoitusehtojen merkityksestä sopimus-vastuussa'. *Defensor Legis* (5/2005): 484–504.

Vuorijoki, Jyrki. 'Todistustaakka sopimuksen syntymisestä ja lakkaamisesta'. *Oikeustieto* (2/1999): 8–9.

Electronic Sources

Association of Finnish Foundations, About Finnish Foundations, https://saatiotrahastot.fi/en/tietoa-saatioista-eng/. Visited on 17 September 2021.

Association of Finnish Foundations, Good Governance of Foundations, https://saatiotrahastot.fi/wp-content/uploads/2021/05/SRNK_Good-Governance-of-Foundations.pdf. Visited on 17 September 2021.

Avtalslagen 2020.se. Visited on 17 September 2021.

Digital and Population Data Services Agency, https://dvv.fi/en/services-of-notary-public. Visited on 29 September 2021.

Finnish Bar Association, http://www.asianajajaliitto.fi. Visited on 29 September 2021.

Finnish Competition and Consumer Authority (Information on the Consumer Ombudsman), https://www.kkv.fi/en/about-us/the-consumer-ombudsman/. Visited on 29 September 2021.

Finnish Patent and Registration Office, https://www.prh.fi/en/saatiorekisteri.html. Visited on 29 September 2021.

Hall Ellis Solicitors, Consideration: Contract Law (Meaning, Types & Purpose), https://hallellis.co.uk/contractual-consideration/. Visited on 29 September 2021.

Investment and Pensions Europe, Finnish Foundation Law Set to Strengthen Governance, https://www.ipe.com/countries/nordic-region/finnish-foundation-law-set-to-strengthen-governance/10011117.article. Visited on 29 September 2021.

Labour Court of Finland, https://www.tyotuomioistuin.fi/en/index.html. Visited on 17 September 2021.

Ministry of Economic Affairs and Employment, Reform of Public Procurement Legislation, http://tem.fi/en/reform-of-public-procurement-legislation. Visited on 29 September 2021.

National Land Survey of Finland, Public Purchase Witnessing, https://www.maanmittauslaitos.fi/en/apartments-and-real-property/real-property-and-property-transactions/public-purchase-witnessing. Visited on 20 September 2021.

Practical Law. A Thomson Reuters Legal Solution, http://uk.practicallaw.com/9-107-6848. Visited on 29 September 2021.

Pro tukipiste, https://protukipiste.fi/ihmiskauppa/tunnista-ihmiskauppa/. Visited on 21 September 2021.

Regional administrative courts, https://oikeus.fi/tuomioistuimet/en/index/tuomioistuinlaitos/tuomioistuimet/hallintotuomioistuimet/hallinto-oikeudet.html. Visited on 17 September 2021.

Roschier Disputes Index 2021, https://www.roschier.com/publications/RDI2021/#p=1. Visited on 29 September 2021.

Supreme Administrative Court, https://www.kho.fi/en/index/organization.html. Visited on 17 September 2021.

The Finland Arbitration Institute, FAI Arbitration Rules, https://arbitration.fi/arbitration/rules/arbitration-rules/. Visited on 29 September 2021.

The Finland Arbitration Institute, FAI Expedited Arbitration Rules, http://arbitration.fi/arbitration/rules/rules-for-expedited-arbitration/. Visited on 29 September 2021.

The Finland Arbitration Institute, Mediation Rules, http://arbitration.fi/mediation/mediation_rules/. Visited on 29 September 2021.

The Finland Arbitration Institute, Model Arbitration Clauses, http://arbitration.fi/arbitration/model-arbitration-clauses/. Visited on 29 September 2021.

Unidroit Principles of International Commercial Contracts 2016, https://www.unidroit.org/wp-content/uploads/2021/06/Unidroit-Principles-2016-English-bl.pdf. Visited on 21 September 2021.

United Nations Commission on International Trade Law, Status: United Nations Convention on Contracts for the international Sale of Goods, https://uncitral.un.org/en/texts/salegoods/conventions/sale_of_goods/cisg/status. Visited on 8 March 2022.

United Nations Information Service, Press Releases 22 May 2012, https://unis.unvienna.org/unis/en/pressrels/2012/unisl162.html. Visited on 29 September 2021.

Selected Bibliography

Index

The numbers here refer to paragraph numbers.

Index

Index